Understanding
Paul

Understanding
Paul

The Early Christian Worldview
of the Letter to the Romans

Second Edition

Stephen Westerholm

Baker Academic
a division of Baker Publishing Group
Grand Rapids, Michigan

© 1997, 2004 by Stephen Westerholm

Published by Baker Academic
a division of Baker Publishing Group
P.O. Box 6287, Grand Rapids, MI 49516-6287
www.bakeracademic.com

First edition published under the title *Preface to the Study of Paul* by William B.
Eerdmans Publishing Company

Printed in the United States of America

                   Library of Congress Cataloging-in-Publication Data
Westerholm, Stephen, 1949–
     Understanding Paul : the early Christian worldview of the letter to the
     Romans / Stephen Westerholm.—2nd ed.
          p.   cm.
     Rev. ed. of: Preface to the study of Paul. Grand Rapids, Mich. : W. B.
Eerdmans Pub., c1997.
     Includes bibliographical references and index.
     ISBN 10: 0-8010-2731-4 (pbk.)
     ISBN 978-0-8010-2731-4 (pbk.)
     1. Bible. N.T. Epistles of Paul—Study and teaching. 2. Bible. N.T. Ro-
mans—Criticism, interpretation, etc. 3. Paul, the Apostle, Saint.
I. Westerholm, Stephen, 1949– Preface to the study of Paul. II. Title.
BS2650.55.W47 2004
227'.106—dc22   2004007268

With love, to
   Jessica, Martin, Paul, and Monica
      —each a gift of Love

Contents

Introduction

Two thousand years later, Paul attracts more attention than any other figure from antiquity but one. Within the academy, anthropological readings of the apostle are heaped upon feminist, which are heaped upon historical, which are heaped upon liberationist or Marxist, which are heaped upon psychological, which are heaped upon rhetorical, which are heaped upon sociological, which are heaped upon theological. One is loath to interrupt such industry. But one can well imagine an outsider—a Herbert, if you will—wanting to pose what to him seems an obvious question: Why Paul?

With all due respect, Herbert doubts that Paul is much better suited to anthropological, psychological, or sociological investigations than many another figure from the ancient world to whom scholars pay little heed. Ancient rhetoric, Herbert confesses, is not, for him, a long-standing interest; but if it were, there are authors he would read before Paul. On the surface, then, the preoccupations of the Pauline industry provide no explanation for its existence. Herbert has, to be sure, his own hunch about what has happened: Paul, important on other grounds, has attracted much—and diverse—scholarly attention. Outsider that he is, Herbert wonders what those other grounds might be. Until he has grasped them and can decide for himself whether they hold any interest, Herbert will tip his hat to the industry—and go his separate way.

Before a client is allowed to escape, however, the industry makes its time-honored pitch. No one (Herbert is assured) did more than Paul for the early spread of Christianity. Letters in his name comprise nearly half the books of the New Testament. His Epistle to the Romans is, by a wide margin, the most influential nonnarrative account of the Christian faith ever written. Its impact on such giants of Western religiosity as Augustine, Luther, Wesley, and Barth has been profound. . . . The litany could continue, but Herbert will have long since broken it off. Everyone knows (vaguely, to be sure, but sufficiently to satisfy themselves on this count) that Paul looms large in the pages of history. The issue remains: Why? What, as Herbert himself would put it, is so big about Paul? What have people seen in him? Why did he make such an impact? Fair questions, all. To satisfy Herbert, we must dig a little deeper.

> Everyone *knows* that Paul looms large in the pages of history. The question is *why?* What is so big about Paul?

Even casual readers of his letters sense that Paul was a man completely captivated by a particular way of looking at life; those who met him must have been similarly struck. Indeed, for many, Paul's captivation proved contagious: the vision of life that Paul communicated gave new direction and significance to their lives as well. It provided them with a sense of what they should and should not do, and motivation for doing what (in the light of the vision) they were convinced was right and worthwhile. In the two millennia since then, Paul's letters have played essentially the same role for millions of readers: they have proved to be a compelling, illuminating, and treasured guide to life.

The record, by any reckoning, is impressive. Few authors can match Paul's staying power; few, the breadth of his readership. Will Herbert be interested? If he is like most of his contemporaries, he has little practice in posing basic questions about life and less education that would encourage him to do so. Confront him with the Socratic claim that "the unexamined life is not worth living," and Herbert's face will register an eloquent blankness: he has nary an inkling how one would examine life or assess the worth of its pursuits. Still, vigorously put, such issues will engage all but the most comatose of readers. And Paul puts them vigorously—none more so: therein, in a nutshell, lie his impact and appeal. Herbert, so informed, can decide for himself whether to take up the challenge or leave it.

Contemporary readers of Paul, however, soon encounter difficulties. Many do not share the assumptions that underlie Paul's vision of life; and to make sense of his train of thought without grasping its premises is no easy matter. Scholars themselves do not always face up to the dilemma. Whatever their intentions, they foster only the parochial arrogance of the modern West if they convey just enough of Paul's thinking (or that of any other ancient) to impress students with its "weirdness." They achieve the same result if they avoid the "weird" and focus only on aspects of Paul's thought related to current notions and concerns. Students, with their unchallenged modern perspective, then simply accept what suits their accustomed ways of thinking and reject the rest—hardly an educational experience!

We have not understood Paul, nor can we judge him fairly, until we have grasped how what repels as well as what attracts us makes sense on his presuppositions. One need not, in the end, be convinced by Paul to comprehend him; one must, at least, see how others could find him convincing. Like all genuine encounters with foreign cultures and ways of thinking, such a stretching of our mental horizons will alert us to presuppositions of our own that we otherwise take for granted.

> One need not be convinced by Paul to comprehend him; but one must at least see how others could find him convincing.

Modern students of Paul's letters need a preface to his thought that addresses the gap between his horizons and their own. In what follows, I allow the argument of Paul's Letter to the Romans to determine both the issues raised and the sequence in which they are handled. Such a procedure should offset the temptation to impose our own systems on Paul's thought or to deal only with aspects of Paul deemed relevant for a modern readership. Discussion (particularly in the early chapters) focuses less on what Paul says than on the assumptions that underlie the text. Topics treated in standard introductions to Romans are here ignored: the dating of the epistle, the beginnings of Christianity in Rome, the character of the Roman Christian community, and the like. Not only is such material readily available elsewhere; until moderns themselves find Paul engaging, such questions are only of academic interest (that is, they are thought worth pursuing only by students who are assured that "they will be on the exam"). The immediate task, then, is to engage. Nor should anyone confuse what follows with a commentary on the details of the epistle. The goal here is to make comprehensible the major components of Paul's vision of life as they are touched upon in his most important letter.

I should perhaps say (the industry will expect it) that the Letter to the Romans *is* a letter, addressed to a particular community at a particular time; it is hardly the sort of document in which one would expect to find a careful, comprehensive statement of Paul's convictions. Some industry spokespeople would want me to add that Paul did not think all that carefully anyway; a few, indeed, believe him to be so incoherent that any project such as mine is misguided. If I must justify proceeding with it, I would say that (1) Romans is a *more* systematic statement of fundamental Pauline convictions than is any other extant letter (presumably because Paul was introducing himself to a community most of whom knew him only by hearsay). (2) Furthermore, while none of us is as coherent as we like to think, I persist in believing that Paul was more so than some of his recent detractors have allowed. That is a thesis, of course, and requires demonstration. What should at least be apparent to all is that the Paul of Romans attempts to place specific issues in a broad context; to relate his convictions to each other, draw out their implications, and answer questions that arise from them. (3) In any case, whether or not *we* find Paul's thinking sensible or coherent, many people over a long period of time have found it compelling. It must be legitimate to ask why.

And so we turn to the thought world of Paul. Surrounded by megamalls, multilayered highways, and multicolored smog, we find it easy to forget that the world of our disguises was once the world of the apostle. So novel are contemporary expressions of the human quest for knowledge, power, gratification, and love that we are tempted to overlook the generic likeness between our lives, still spanning threescore years and ten, and his. Yet apologists of the modern age who see history as a one-way street of unimpeded progress are fewer today than they were scant decades ago. Realistic scorecards pitting the contemporary scene against that of bygone eras now show losses as well as gains;

and so they must, if we are not to forget entire dimensions of the human experience.

But to keep an honest score, we must study the past for purposes other than to satisfy antiquarian curiosity or to fuel the indignation of modern ideologies. More demanding of our patience and imagination is the task of reconstructing the world as it once appeared, and made sense, to our fellow human beings. Yet academics fail their generation if they do not transmit such alternative visions against which moderns may measure their own. Within the world as Paul described it, millions of people for two millennia have lived and found meaningful the vicissitudes of their lives. It is a vision, one can only conclude, with sufficient cogency and depth to intrigue and challenge moderns as well—provided they are equipped to understand it.

1

The Commission and Its Context

Romans 1:1–15

The opening of Romans offers nothing to cheer those who would fain believe that even Paul must, on occasion, have engaged in small talk. At the outset he presents himself as a man under commission, briefly defines his assigned task, then declares that he has long desired to meet his readers in person—for the rather *im*personal reason that they, too, fall within the sphere of his mandate. Toward the end of the letter Paul indicates that he is writing in order to discharge apostolic responsibilities among the Romans that circumstances had kept him from fulfilling by other means.[1] In short, the only Paul we encounter in Romans is one acting consciously in what he regarded as his appointed office: that of an "apostle."

1. See Romans 15:15–22.

Our interest here is in seeing the world through Paul's (ever so apostolic) eyes: in grasping something of the way Paul came to view, and convinced others to view, the nature and terms of human existence. But in these opening verses, he provides only a brief summary of *what* it is that he communicates to others, using terms ("gospel of God," "Son of God," "resurrection from the dead") that we may more conveniently explore when they become central to his argument. What dominates the introduction is not the substance of Paul's message but the claim that he has been commissioned to promote it. This sense of mission—the sense that he has been given a significant part to play in a drama that is nonetheless much bigger than he is—surfaces constantly in Paul's writings. We do well to begin, as he begins Romans, with his apostolic self-understanding.

> Paul, a servant of Jesus Christ, called to be an apostle, set apart for the gospel of God . . .
>
> Through [Jesus Christ] we have received grace and apostleship to bring about the obedience of faith among all the Gentiles.
>
> I am a debtor both to Greeks and to barbarians, both to the wise and to the foolish—hence my eagerness to proclaim the gospel to you also who are in Rome.
>
> Romans 1:1, 5, 14–15 NRSV

A Man under Commission

Unsympathetic readings of Paul tend to characterize him as self-important, authoritarian, opinionated, and intolerant. Paul would have responded with an apostolic huff—and, from his perspective, with good reason. Self-important? What can we expect of a man convinced, first, that he lived at the turning point in the conflict of the ages between good and evil, and, second, that through a role-casting that surprised no one more than himself, he had been entrusted with the task of enlisting the non-Jews of the world on the side of the good. Not all will think the drama credible; none can fault one who found it so for playing his part to the hilt. Authoritarian? In all fairness, we should note that Paul was not as rigid on some issues as he was on most. Even in the latter cases, he justified his firmness with appeals, not to his prerogatives as an apostle, but to reasons that he believed mattered to his readers as well as to himself. We can add that he never exempted himself from any constraint or sacrifice that he imposed on others. That being said, we may agree that Paul showed a singular aptitude for demanding compliance. Yet we should also agree that *some* jobs require such a facility; and Paul's own task—as he understood both it and the stakes it involved—must surely be reckoned among them.

Opinionated? Intolerant? Again, such captions are flatly contradicted by *parts* of the evidence. And when Paul was as inflexible as only he could be, he would, in his own mind, have betrayed his commission if he had acted differently. Nor would he have allowed that the matters on which he insisted were his own opinions. At issue, as he saw things, were truths that he had been obliged to accept in the light of his commissioning. Loyalty to an awesome task, for which he would be held awesomely responsible, required him to uphold them. He did so—one must concede—with admirable vigor.

The *root* of the problem that many people today have with Paul is thus not our distaste for his self-importance, authoritarianism, or intolerance. Instead, it is our (perhaps subconscious) penchant for discounting a claim to which we are not inclined to give credence: that the resurrected "Son of God" had commissioned Paul. The contemporary dismissal of this particular claim can be placed in a wider context: the worldview of many people today will not admit of revelation from any supernatural source. Paul's convictions were not so constricted. If, then, we assume that what makes

> Nowhere is Paul's sense that he had been commissioned as an apostle more apparent than in Galatians 1:
>
> Paul an apostle—sent neither by human commission nor from human authorities, but through Jesus Christ and God the Father, who raised him from the dead. ... I want you to know, brothers and sisters, that the gospel that was proclaimed by me is not of human origin; for I did not receive it from a human source, nor was I taught it, but I received it through a revelation of Jesus Christ. ... God, who had set me apart before I was born and called me through his grace, was pleased to reveal his Son to me, so that I might proclaim him among the Gentiles.
>
> Galatians 1:1, 11–12, 15–16 NRSV

no sense to us cannot have been meant seriously by Paul, we only betray our own cultural blinders.

That Paul himself was convinced that the resurrected Christ had commissioned him is apparent on several counts: from the redirection of his life that his conviction occasioned (the prudence of the worldly wise could not, in Paul's day, have prompted the change from foe to champion of the Christian cause); from the energy he devoted to the fulfillment of his commission; from the fervor of the religious convictions Paul held because he believed he had seen God's "son"; from his loyalty to both commission and convictions in the face of hardship and death. In his own mind, Paul was an authorized representative of Jesus Christ. And he applied himself to his august task with a passion and a single-mindedness so remarkable that his readers have been left in doubt whether the man was even pervious to the charms of small talk.

The Framework of the Commission

The problem remains: How are people today to enter the thought world of someone who was convinced that he had experienced what their own worldview excludes as impossible? This difficulty will occupy us throughout the pages that follow. Still, an initial sketch of a pathway into Paul's world—filled in with more detail in following chapters—may help us understand how Paul's commission would be seen from within his own horizons.

Newspapers commonly report that a happy, healthy, vivacious child was kidnapped, abused, murdered. We cannot but wonder, on reading such stories, what kind of world we inhabit. Of the many answers that could be given, I will briefly summarize two as a reminder that the same events are susceptible of different interpretations, then consider a third perspective at somewhat greater length as our entrée into the thought world of Paul.

1. The vibrant, innocent life of a child is rightly valued by humans; we deplore its brutal curtailment. Such incidents reveal the utter indifference of the universe to the values and sensibilities of human beings. The world continues on its chaotic way after, as before, a child's life is snuffed out. Apart

from humans, "all that is" is only a purposeless conglomerate of matter. Value and meaning are exclusively the products of human intelligence, feeling, and will. Yet human possibilities of imposing order on reality are quite limited. Inevitably, cold, indifferent nature wins in the end. We can only affirm—in no one's hearing but our own—that our efforts have made the interval worthwhile.

2. The child's life was good, its curtailment evil. Human history represents only one of the battlefields on which eternally opposed, superhuman forces wage their constant struggle: powers of creation and destruction, order and chaos, life and death, goodness and evil.

3. The life of a child is good, a precious gift and cause for celebration. So, each in its own right, is the life of the great horned owl, the bay-breasted wood warbler, the great northern pike, and the yellow damselfish. That there are harlequin tuskfish and shingle-back skinks is good, whether or not humans are aware of their existence. Indeed, all that is, because it is and because it has a part in all-that-is, is good. Humans themselves are but a part of all-that-is, distinctive as each species is distinct, but too obviously related to the rest of creation to imagine that they alone give it meaning or worth. Like many another species, they are born, then sustained in early life by those to whom they owe their birth; they grow in stature and in knowledge; they learn to procure their livelihood; they love and are loved; they couple, reproduce, then care—at great sacrifice to themselves—for the new life with which they have been entrusted. We are but a part of this world. It is not of our design or making, nor are we the source of its goodness. For that we must look to the great Lover of life and beauty, who is eternal and good.

Yet children are murdered in this world. It does not follow that the cosmos is itself without value and indifferent to goodness; only that it has become the scene of much that is evil. The evil is real: neither good (like the life of a child) nor evil (like the murder of a child) exists only in human minds. Evil is that which resists and disrupts what is good. Yet evil is not, like good, eternal. By its very resistant, disruptive nature, evil is parasitic: it cannot exist apart from the good—to which it responds inappropriately. We live neither in a world to which we alone bring value, nor in one in which good and evil are coequal combatants. Our world is essentially and wonderfully good, but profoundly and horribly disturbed by things that ought never, and need never, have occurred.

> For Paul (and other early Christians), our world is essentially and wonderfully good, but profoundly and horribly disturbed by things that ought never, and need never, have occurred.

All three interpretations (and others could, of course, be cited) provide a framework within which one can understand the murder of a child. They conflict and cannot all be true on any fundamental level (though, in principle, they could all be false).[2] We may be inclined to conclude that, given the plethora of possible interpretations, our attempts to arrive at the truth of such matters are pointless: better to content ourselves with the demands and satisfactions of life immediately before us. But such is an impoverished human existence—and it is not academic arrogance that labels it so. The academic may lament that Kant, Kierkegaard, and Camus are too little read, believing that familiarity with their work can enrich our human experience. But we need not be academics to realize that, without *some* framework, without *some* vision of what life is about, we have no explanation for why we do what we do; no resource for distinguishing worthwhile pursuits from others that are trivial; no basis for answering the moral questions of a child; no language for articulating the significance of turning points in our lives; no nonsedative means for coping with tragedy. None of us ever does live without *some* kind of interpretive framework. But we differ widely in the degree of thoughtfulness with which we live, the consistency with which we approach the various aspects of our lives, the coherence of the framework that—consciously or unconsciously—we find ourselves adopting.

2. The conceit that *no* human construction corresponds to reality represents a fashionably self-contradictory version of the first interpretation: construing reality as chaotic, it declares that no construction of reality can be true. If, however, reality *has* meaningful order, as the sages of other ages have believed, then there is no obvious reason why the human mind, itself a fragment of the whole, cannot capture a glimpse of the latter's awesome symmetry. On any reading, human perceptions never exhaust reality.

We need some framework; at certain levels, most any framework will serve. But human curiosity, our insatiable capacity to wonder and question, will demand at some point whether the framework that we have adopted is *true;* whether our pursuits are worthwhile in any forum other than that of our own imaginings; whether we are answering or only pacifying the queries of a child. We can hardly

> Without *some* vision of what life is about, we have no resource for distinguishing worthwhile pursuits from ones that are trivial, no basis for answering the moral questions of a child, no nonsedative means for coping with tragedy.

pose such questions of any framework until we have a fair grasp of the framework as a whole and of how things look from within its boundaries. Only then can we ask whether such a way of viewing life is coherent, whether it can do justice to all that we know of human experience, whether it gives value to what we sense must be valued, and so on. These are essential, human questions, but they lie beyond our purview here. Our more limited goal is the preliminary one of finding a basis for understanding a particular vision, widely influential—though now widely forgotten.

The Appropriateness of the Commission

Paul's vision of reality is, of course, one version of the third interpretation sketched above. Such a summary provokes myriads of doubts and queries: How can evil originate in a world supposedly good? How can a God supposedly good permit it to happen? How does one explain the existence, not only of moral evil, but also of natural disasters? These questions all have their place. But our immediate concern in this chapter is how a commission such as Paul believed he had received, though incredible to many people today, made sense to him.

If nonhuman reality has no value of its own, and if the only order it shows is mechanical, then Paul's commission as he understood it is impossible.[3] But things look quite different to the

---

3. Indeed, if we are to maintain such an interpretive framework, we must refuse credence to any and every claim of religious experience. None can be ac-

Jewish or Christian mind. If all-that-is, including the Source of
all-that-is, is in its essence good, then evil is both a disruption
of what-is and an affront to its Source. Yet the Source of all-
that-is surely has the resources to deal with such disruptions.
Moreover, being by nature good, God will not be inclined to
ignore the appearance and threat
of evil. If creation's goodness has
been marred, then a good Creator
can be counted on to do something
about it.

> According to Acts 9, Paul (or
> "Saul," as he is initially called in
> Acts) was approaching Damascus
> when "suddenly a light from
> heaven flashed around him. He
> fell to the ground and heard a
> voice saying to him, 'Saul, Saul,
> why do you persecute me?' He
> asked, 'Who are you, Lord?' The
> reply came, 'I am Jesus, whom
> you are persecuting. But get up
> and enter the city, and you will be
> told what you are to do.'"
>
> Acts 9:3–6 NRSV

So much seems clear; but more
follows. If God gave creation its
order in the first place, then God is
not likely, without a good reason,
to interfere with nature's order by
acting in miraculous ways. Still,
one good reason why God *might*
choose to act miraculously would
be to draw the attention of unsus-
pecting human beings to what he
is doing about the evil in his world.
When Paul set out for Damascus,
he did not expect to meet the risen

Christ. Still, he knew what to make of such a happening: extraordinary it was, but hardly incredible. Far more incredible
for Paul would have been the suggestion that the God of life
and love would permit evil to encroach uninterrupted on the
goodness of his creation. To Paul's mind, then, the startling way
in which he was charged with his mandate was only suited to
its import: to proclaim God's stunning response to evil and the
decisive triumph of the Good.

In the chapters that follow, we will attempt to retrieve the
vision of life worked out by Paul in the light of what he believed
to be a divine revelation and commissioning. One further aspect of the task itself warrants mention here. Paul's mission,
as he saw it, was to the world's non-Jews (or "Gentiles"). The

---

cepted on its own terms; all must be given nonreligious explanations. Religious
people themselves are wont to see here a weakness in a mechanical, naturalistic
worldview.

presumption that humanity can be meaningfully categorized as "Jews" and "all the rest" is itself telling of the way Paul thought. Note, further, that for Paul the movement of truth was *from* Jews *to* all the rest: initially it pertained to Jews in so real a sense that its later spread to Gentiles put the latter in the former's debt.[4] More is meant than that events of great importance had just taken place among Jews. Rather, important recent events were seen as the climax of a whole series of events involving God and the Jews; and Jews had been given the key to understanding what God was up to.[5] The intended beneficiaries included all nations, and, ultimately, all creation;[6] but Jews were seen as the people through whom others would be blessed. Much of the dynamics of Romans is provided by Paul's dual insistence on (1) the universal goal of the "gospel of God" and (2) the continuing need to be faithful to its Jewish character and roots.

Far better than most of his contemporaries, Paul knew the eastern half of the Roman Empire. He lived and worked in a number of its cities. He could not have communicated with its inhabitants as effectively as he did if he had not known their language, customs, hopes, and fears. Nor can we proceed far in the study of his letters without needing to take into account the occurrence of terms, techniques, and notions drawn from his familiarity with the Greco-Roman world. Still, the exploration of such details lies beyond our purpose here. The underlying framework remains, for Paul, Jewish in its origins. It includes his convictions about the goodness of God the Creator and the derived goodness of the created order; an understanding of creation's present *dis*order, not in tragic terms, as the surfacing of flaws or tensions inherent in the cosmos itself, but in moral and religious terms, as the consequence of creaturely unfaithfulness toward God; the implacable hostility of God toward the evil that mars the goodness of what he has made; the ultimate triumph of the Good assured by the combination of God's own irrepressible goodness and his irresistible right arm. Paul's Christian understanding of divine redemption fits perfectly within

4. Romans 1:16; 15:27.
5. See Romans 1:2; 3:1–2; also 15:4.
6. See Romans 3:29–30; 8:21; 11:32.

these horizons, though it certainly required modifications of other Jewish beliefs. Our task in the pages that follow will be to recover the main lines of Paul's distinctive statement of this "Jewish-Christian" worldview.[7]

7. The "Jewish-Christian" worldview referred to here and in the pages that follow is that defined, as in the paragraph above, by the following convictions: God is good, and so is his creation; evil represents an inappropriate and disruptive response on the part of moral beings to what is good; the triumph of the Good is ultimately assured by the character of God. That Judaism and Christianity have developed in quite different ways, with different emphases, may well be obscured by unqualified references to a "Jewish-Christian" tradition or heritage. The Jewish origin of the central Christian (and Pauline) convictions listed above is the sole point of my own references to the "Jewish-Christian" worldview. (The quotation marks are intended to limit the term to the technical sense here defined.)

2

Intuitions of Goodness— and Divine *Tzedakah*

Romans 1:16–17

That life—all life—is meaningful and good, and that evil distorts and disrupts the good and cries out to be set right: these convictions are fundamental to the "Jewish-Christian" worldview,[1] of which Paul is a notable exponent. They are not self-evident today. In this chapter a general discussion of the differences in horizons will be followed by a look at the theme of underlying goodness in the biblical book of Psalms. We will then see, in conclusion, how that vision provides the framework for the Pauline manifesto in Romans 1:16–17.

Love—and the Nature of Things

We may begin with a parable.

Barb and Bob knew each other for years before they "discovered" one another. The details of the discovery need not concern

1. On the phrase, see chapter 1, note 7.

us here. Barb and Bob themselves feel that what has happened to them is utterly unique in the annals of human history, and in a sense, of course, they are right: Barb is unique, so is Bob, and so perforce must be their relationship. But though we grant the point with goodwill—we were, after all, once young ourselves—we do them no injustice when we insist that, broadly speaking, what has happened to them *has* happened to others before; that for all its novelty in detail, there is a certain predictability about many aspects of their relationship; that the whole experience is sufficiently common in sufficiently significant ways to warrant the dusting off of a well-worn tag: Barb and Bob have "fallen in love," and even those who know neither Barb nor Bob, when they hear the news, have a fair idea of what has taken place.

Indeed, whether or not Barb and Bob care to acknowledge it, their mutual discovery bears an unmistakable resemblance to that of a male and female albatross whom we will call Jack and Jill. Jill, on returning to the land of her birth, is beset by many males, all craving her attention; but she finds herself attracted to Jack. A certain formality of gesture and speech, both awkward and tense with excitement, characterizes their initial introductions: their attachment will be lifelong, but its beginnings must not be rushed. Introductions are followed by gentle caressing, then a dance—formal, predictable, yet reaching a feverish ecstasy before subsiding into the contentment of the mutual knowledge that they are a pair. Still, Jack and Jill separate for a season without mating. Their reunion is marked again by both excitement and formality, though now, at the end of their courtship dance, they mate, then prepare to take up the shared responsibilities of parenting.

We leave them to their duties and return to Barb and Bob. Their new relationship has transformed their lives. Their pursuit of work and education is now purposeful, focused on making possible their life together. The tritest of occasions has taken on meaning—provided they can share it with each other. Even separation from one another differs from times they used to spend on their own: absence is not the same as aloneness. Nor would we be mistaken in thinking Barb and Bob more beautiful human beings than they were before: more happy, certainly, but also more generous, more patient, more considerate. That love is blind, attributing spectacular virtues to spectacularly ordinary people, is not, after all, the whole truth. Love may also summon virtue into being.

So much for the parable. In view of the pluralism—the *multi*culturalism—of our society, you would not, of course, permit that the story be given but a single interpretation. Will . . . *two* do?

On one view,[2] Barb and Bob are in the process of inventing the terms of their own relationship. Others have had similar experiences; human physiology has seen to that. Still, in a mechanical universe whose only meaning or value is human in origin, nothing in the accidents of human physiology or in the experience of other human beings can dictate to our pair what *their* attitudes or behavior ought to be. Admittedly, some things that they might choose to do will lead to predictable consequences, and we would not think them wise to overlook such factors when they make their choices. Some of their potential activities impinge upon society as a whole; in such matters they will need to take into account the law of the land (they must, for example, assume responsibility for any offspring). Still, if humans are autonomous—if they are on their own, so to speak, in the universe—pursuing their own ends in a value-neutral world, then Barb and Bob are largely free to make (and break) their own rules, to create a relationship that suits only them, and to enjoy it as long as they mutually choose to do so.

But for many people of other lands and ages (and for many people still today), the suggestion that Barb and Bob are inventing something new in an unstructured, value-free universe would be counterintuitive and nonsensical. The intuitions of such people are guided in part by widespread familiarity with what Barb and Bob have experienced (indeed, the pattern, as we have noted, extends beyond humans to include Jack and Jill Albatross as well). People of the modern West may be inclined to dismiss the significance of the pattern, attributing it to the accidents of animal physiology and insisting that, at any rate, Barb and Bob must be left free to create the terms of their own

2. The point of view here summarized is chosen because (1) it is common enough in our day, and (2) it offers a sharp and illuminating contrast to the thinking of Paul. That there are other and intermediary positions is not denied; but it lies outside my purpose to develop them.

relationship, to determine what is best for themselves. Historically, however, many people, observing animal and human physiology and its transparent fittedness for the perpetuation of species, have seen evidence of a design in nature—and of the wisdom of a designer. They have sensed, further, that a design that underlies and defines the nature of our being must place limits on what behavior is fitting, or most fulfilling, for human beings. To this latter point we will return in due course.

For our immediate purposes, however, an even more crucial intuition than that of design has been that of nature's inherent goodness. Barb and Bob's love is not only nature's convenient way of assuring the propagation of the species. It is itself a Good Thing, a cause for celebration in its own right. Nor has its goodness been thought of as confined to that of sensual pleasure (though sensual pleasure belongs to its more obvious enticements and rewards). Indeed, the goodness of love is commonly considered to be more purely expressed, and more lastingly felt, in the mutual support of lovers through the monotonies of quotidian tasks and the pains and struggles of hard times.

> According to one worldview, lovers are free to invent the terms of their own relationship. According to another, the design that underlies and defines the nature of our being places limits on what behavior is fitting, or most fulfilling, for human beings.

Furthermore, if the awakening of a human being to the reality and goodness of another's existence and the subordinating of individual goals and interests to the higher values of mutuality are Good Things, then the same must presumably be said of Jack and Jill's adoption of a life with a similar pattern. Humans may bring to their experience a degree of consciousness and a capacity for articulation that *this* Jack and Jill will never possess; but the latter, too, know, delight in, and sacrifice for the goodness of a shared existence. In short, humans (and other species of animals) appear to many to have been designed in such a way as to entice them to the goodness of mutuality: "It is not good that the man should be alone."[3] We can, on this interpretation, only rejoice that Barb and Bob have come to discover and experience

3. Genesis 2:18 NRSV.

something fundamental to the nature of their humanity. But (still on this interpretation) we can only shake our heads at their hubris if they imagine that they are themselves the creators of purpose and goodness in a structureless, value-free universe.

According to the first view, we live in a world thrown together by the chance assembly of particles of matter. The suitedness to survival that we discern in its life-forms must represent, not the work of some supernatural designer, but merely those random combinations of globules that have proved capable of perpetuating themselves. To speak of the beauty or goodness of all-that-is or of any of its parts is merely a poetic (or naive) way of saying that certain conglomerations of globules seem pleasing or useful to us. Furthermore, humans are completely free to reshape what nature has thrown together into something that better suits their tastes or convenience; after all, a nature with no purpose of its own provides only raw material for purpose-driven human beings. Nor can there be any inherent rightness or wrongness in the nature of things, haphazard and unstructured as things are.

In principle, then, humans are free to choose what they think best or most desirable for themselves. Since their choices will be diverse, the greatest premium will be placed on the virtue of tolerance (that is, on our ability to live with people who choose differently than we), whereas a great vice will be seen in any attempt to impose one's own choices on others. Any constraint placed upon us not of our choosing (apart from those required for mutual coexistence) can only be an arbitrary, unjustifiable expression of a "will to power," a desire to dominate, on the part of the constrainer. (People whose thinking is governed by such a worldview can only view would-be apostles with grave suspicion!)

On the second worldview sketched above, however, trouble springs precisely from the human presumption that we are free to remake the world to our own specifications, that nature itself has no order or goodness that we need to respect. Words like "beauty" and "goodness," while reflecting human perceptions, put us on the right track: they express an awareness of a presence and purpose in nature not our own, to which we appropriately respond with wonder and appreciation. Nor, on this view, can the language of right and wrong, at its root, be the sheer invention of human beings who want to impose their will on others. However subject to abuse and distortion such language may be, it is nonetheless grounded in a proper sense that there are adequate and inadequate, appropriate and disastrously inappropriate, ways of responding to the reality of life in our world.

Obviously, human choice is pivotal to this worldview, as it is to the first. According to the first view, humans choose how to shape an unstructured world to their liking. But according to the second view, the distinctiveness of human beings lies in their capacity to grasp, affirm, and celebrate the already-existing goodness of the created order. They are thus called upon to add a peculiarly *human* dimension to the goodness and glory of the whole. Yet, alas, the capacity for affirming and celebrating the good inevitably opens to humans the contrary possibility as well: they *can* refuse to acknowledge or respect any good in the cosmos but that of personal ambition and pleasure. The self-absorption of the latter choice breeds rivalry, distrust, conflict, and destruction.

> Trouble springs precisely from the human presumption that we are free to remake the world to our own specifications, that nature itself has no order or goodness that we need to respect.

The worldviews here sketched are in fundamental tension with each other. Contemporary confidence that the scientific method can resolve the dispute is misplaced. Science may observe nature's conduciveness to various kinds of life, but it has no instrument for determining whether life is good. Science may note the patterns or the chaos apparent in the fraction of reality open to its observation. Yet its grasp of all-that-is can never be sufficient to justify claims about the structure, or lack of structure, of the whole. Nor, if there is structure, can the observations of science distinguish between a mechanically functioning order and an intelligently formed design. Science can tell us how to exploit nature; it is silent about the extent to which we should. To evaluate the fundamental human issues raised by a comparison of worldviews, we need to summon human resources both deeper and older than the scientific method.

The Goodness That Underlies All—in the Psalms

In the book of Psalms, we repeatedly encounter the insistence that "the LORD is good"; we are even offered the exquisite invitation to "taste and see" how good he is.[4] One might think that God is simply good by definition: Is it not, after all, a prerogative of the Creator to decide what is good and what is bad in the first place? Still, the psalmists believed that they were making a significant statement. Frequently they have in mind the kindness shown by the Lord to those in need. Psalm 107 summons all humanity to praise the Lord for his goodness, and develops the point by declaring that he comes to the aid of the lost, the imprisoned, the sick and hungry, the storm-tossed. In short, those in need who cry out to the Lord are believed to experience firsthand his goodness.[5]

The psalmists believe that God's goodness is also, and more fundamentally, reflected in creation itself, in the goodness of life in a world perceived as splendidly and benevolently ordered.[6] The

> The earth is full of the dependable love of the LORD.
>
> Psalm 33:5

chaotic seas have been put in their place, thank God![7] So have the mountains, and they are not about to move anywhere, praise the Lord![8] The springs and the valleys, the grass and the trees all have *their* place.[9] So do animals, storm winds, rain, snow and hail, the sun, the moon, and all the stars; indeed, God has given to each of the stars not only a place but also a name.[10] All is perfectly ordered and providentially sustained. The world, we are told, is "full of the dependable love of the LORD."[11]

We may well find curious the way the psalmists can abstract, out of all the ambiguities of lived experience, this *un*ambiguous

---

4. Psalm 34:8. Biblical references use the numbering of chapters and verses found in standard English versions.
5. See also Psalm 31:19; 86:5.
6. See Psalm 65:9–13; 104:27–28; 145:9–10.
7. See Psalm 33:7; 65:7; 89:9.
8. See Psalm 65:6; 104:5–9.
9. Psalm 104:10–17.
10. Psalm 147:4; 148:3–10.
11. Psalm 33:5.

portrayal of the glories of the created order. The psalmists knew
famine, disease, violence, and death. And yet, in some of the
psalms at least, no trace of evil of any kind is part of the picture.
The focus, the single-mindedness, the purity of their vision is
impressive. On a similar note, the psalmists boldly summon humanity of all shapes and sizes and ages and nations to respond
with appropriate praise to the Lord. Yet in their day, the "Lord"
was acknowledged and worshiped only by the people of a petty
kingdom of the Levant, themselves not always exclusive in their
devotion. Nothing of this clouds the psalmists' horizons.

> Kings of the earth, and all people;
>   princes, and all judges of the earth:
> Both young men, and maidens;
>   old men, and children:
> Let them praise the name of the Lord:
>   for his name alone is excellent.[12]

To dismiss such texts as naive would only show our own naivety.
Rather, they are an affirmation that ultimately, fundamentally,
creation is good and the Creator deserving of universal praise;
that the reality of evil is not ultimate but secondary and parasitic,
a disorder brought about by inappropriate responses to the goodness of the fundamental order. Consequently, the psalmists were
determined that, for the moment at least, they were not going to
allow secondary distractions, however distressing, or the blindness
of others, however widespread or obtuse, to interfere with their
celebration of the essential goodness of life in God's creation.

Still more fundamentally, the psalmists found good, and profoundly satisfying, not simply the manifest works of the Lord,
but also, and at a deeper level, a sense of his very presence. To
worship in the courtyard of the Lord's temple was for them to
experience his goodness in an exhilarating, almost palpable way,
so that a single day there was treasured more than a thousand
anywhere else.[13] There one "beheld" the Lord's "beauty" and
"sang for joy" to the "living God."[14] To "dwell in the house of
the Lord for ever" was to know "goodness and mercy" all one's

12. Psalm 148:11–13 KJV.
13. Psalm 84:10; also 65:4.
14. Psalm 27:4; 84:2.

days.[15] Separation from God's house left one faint, longing as a deer for flowing streams, parched as in a "dry and weary land."[16] It provoked the cry:

> O send out your light and your truth;
> > let them lead me;
> let them bring me to your holy hill
> > and to your dwelling.
> Then will I go to the altar of God,
> > to God my exceeding joy;
> and I will praise you with the harp,
> > O God, my God.[17]

The writer of the incomparable Psalm 139 goes further: the divine presence encompasses him wherever he may go.

> If I take the wings of the morning,
> > and dwell in the uttermost parts of the sea;
> Even there shall thy hand lead me,
> > and thy right hand shall hold me. . . .
> When I awake, I am still with thee.[18]

Again, the psalmists who found such satisfaction in God's "face" were fully aware of the darker aspects of life: is there anywhere a literature that more profoundly probes the lot of the despised, the slandered, the despondent, those ravaged by disease or war? God's ways are often disturbingly mysterious even for the psalmists. They feel that at times he has "hidden" his "face," and they cannot understand why.[19] Nonetheless, what prevails in the end is the unshakable faith in their bones, whatever the fate of their flesh, that underlying all is goodness, beyond human understanding but deserving of human trust: a goodness not only worth clinging to when all else fails, but more precious by far than anything else one might desire.

15. So ends the familiar Psalm 23 KJV.
16. Psalm 42:1; 63:1.
17. Psalm 43:3–4 NRSV.
18. Psalm 139:9–10, 18 KJV.
19. Psalm 13:1; 89:46.

> Whom have I in heaven but you?
>   And there is nothing on earth
>   that I desire other than you.
>   My flesh and my heart may fail,
>   but God is the strength of my heart
>   and my portion forever.[20]

Divine goodness cannot, however, fail in the end, nor remain ambiguous forever: divine *tzedakah* will see to that. This Hebrew word is commonly translated "righteousness," a term that captures part of what the psalmists mean to convey: God keeps his word and lives up to his obligations, which include enforcing the moral order, seeing to it that both righteous and wicked receive their due recompense. But the term *righteousness* has fallen into disuse and does not in any case sufficiently suggest the element of *goodness* so obviously present in psalmic texts that summon the universe to celebrate God's *tzedakah*. In such verses *tzedakah* refers to the faithfulness of God toward his creation or his people, a faithfulness that moves him to intervene, to set things wonderfully right when they have gone disastrously awry. It is the reassertion of God's goodness seen in the restoration of just order to a disturbed creation, of peace and prosperity to a distressed people. In this sense *tzedakah* is close in meaning to *salvation*. What *tzedakah* adds to the "reassertion of goodness" and even "salvation" is the implication that God, in the process, is living up to his responsibility and role as God. He is proving himself loyal to the commitments he undertook when he first made the world good or adopted Israel as his people.

> Underlying all is goodness, beyond human understanding but deserving of human trust: a goodness more precious by far than anything else one might desire.

> O sing unto the LORD a new song;
>   for he hath done marvelous things:
>   his right hand, and his holy arm,
>   hath gotten him the victory.

---

20. Psalm 73:25–26 NRSV.

The LORD hath made known his salvation:
　his righteousness [*tzedakah*] hath he openly showed
　　in the sight of the heathen.
He hath remembered his mercy and his truth
　toward the house of Israel:
　all the ends of the earth have seen
　the salvation of our God. . . .
Let the sea roar, and the fullness
　　thereof;
　the world, and they that dwell
　　therein.
Let the floods clap their hands:
　let the hills be joyful together
Before the LORD; for he cometh
　to judge the earth:
　with righteousness [*tzedek*]
　　shall he judge the world,
and the people with equity.[21]

> *Tzedakah* is the faithfulness and goodness of God, on display whenever God restores just order to his disturbed creation, or peace and prosperity to his distressed people.

Similar uses of the term *tzedakah* (also in close parallel with "salvation") occur in the later chapters of Isaiah, as the prophet proclaims how a despondent people in exile are about to experience afresh the divine goodness.[22] In speaking of the proclamation of such good news, the prophet uses a verb translated in Greek as *euangelizesthai*,[23] related to the noun *euangelion* (whence the English word *evangelist*), which, in turn, appears in the English New Testament as "gospel."

. . . and in Paul

When Paul, in turning from his commission to "proclaim good news" (*euangelisasthai*)[24] to a summary manifesto of what it is he proclaims, declares that the "gospel (*euangelion*)" brings God's "salvation" and demonstrates di-

> For I am not ashamed of the gospel; it is the power of God for salvation to everyone who has faith, to the Jew first and also to the Greek. For in it the righteousness of God is revealed through faith for faith; as it is written, "The one who is righteous will live by faith."
>
> **Romans 1:16–17** NRSV

21. Psalm 98:1–3, 7–9 KJV.
22. Isaiah 45:8; 46:12–13; 51:6.
23. Isaiah 40:9; 52:7; 61:1; as in Romans 15:20.
24. Romans 1:15.

vine "righteousness,"[25] he is interpreting the significance of Jesus within the framework provided by the Jewish vision of divine goodness sketched in this chapter. God is good, and so, necessarily, is his creation. His *tzedakah*[26] demands that, in a world gone awry, God will restore, in some manifestly divine fashion, the goodness of what he has made.

25. Romans 1:16–17.
26. The term in Hebrew has taken on a more limited sense: human liberality, almsgiving, charity. I use the term in the sense given it in the cited passages from the Psalms and Isaiah (above).

3

War against Goodness

Romans 1:18–32

No doubt each of us has a partiality for one or more of the seven deadly sins; still, the term *sin* itself has largely dropped out of our vocabulary. We begin this chapter with reflections about the contemporary discomfort with, and a possible approach to, "Jewish-Christian"[1] notions of wrongdoing. We will then look briefly at the morality of the biblical book of Proverbs before focusing on significant features of Paul's own depiction of human sin in Romans 1:18–32.

Doubts about "Sin"

The very notion of wrongdoing is approached by many people today with misgivings. Several contributing factors are worth noting.

1. In Western societies we insist on the freedom of individuals to choose for themselves, to pursue their own goals and values.

---

1. On the term, see chapter 1, note 7.

Complete freedom of choice we know to be impractical in a
world whose air we must share with others (that is, in the world
as we know it, we need to take some account of others' needs
and desires at the same time as we pursue the satisfaction of our
own) and whose surface, should we test it by a leap from any
great height, provides little cushion (that is, in the world as we
know it, a consideration of predictable consequences will, for
most of us, quickly exclude a fair number of potential choices).
Nonetheless, we remain suspicious of attempts to restrict our
options. Many people today resist the assertion of traditional
morality that certain ways in which they might choose to express
themselves are inherently wrong.

2. Closely related is the contemporary insistence that people
must not impose their moral standards or values on others or
be judgmental. Again, the implication seems to be that it is not
for any of us to say that what other people choose to do is right
or wrong.

3. Historically, religious conviction was one of the roots of our
society's insistence on individual freedom. In the beginnings of
the American experiment, for ex-
ample, a central element was the
demand of different groups to be
allowed to worship as they deemed
right. At issue for them was not
whether there *was* a right way to
worship (the answer to this question tended to be yes), but whether
the powers-that-be in the land-
that-was had rightly divined it (the
answer to this question tended to
be no). Right and wrong there were. But where citizens believed
themselves to be in the right and their rulers to be in the wrong,
constraints imposed by the latter upon the former were liable
to be seen as violating their conscience; hence the fervor with
which they demanded freedom to worship as *they* deemed one
should worship.

To be sure, these groups themselves were not always willing to
extend freedom of worship to others who disagreed with them.
In time, however, most came to see that religious beliefs and
moral conduct, if they are to represent truly religious or moral

> The very notion of wrongdoing
> is approached by many people
> today with misgivings. Many resist
> traditional morality's assertion
> that certain ways in which
> they might choose to express
> themselves are inherently wrong.

acts, must be freely chosen by the individual; they cannot be the result of mere compliance with the state's demands. There is thus, in the demand for freedom in matters of both faith and morals, nothing either in principle or in its history inconsistent with firm beliefs that there are rights to be chosen and wrongs to be avoided.

Nonetheless, in societies where a diversity of conviction is permitted and no particular perspective on matters of religion or morals is allowed a platform in public institutions, the language of right and wrong that characterizes strongly held convictions easily comes to appear ill-suited to public discourse—and suspect in people's minds. Children taught in religious homes about the fundamental importance of religious beliefs and practices, and of religiously grounded moral standards, can hardly avoid wondering how fundamental such matters can be when they are either studiously avoided in the classroom or brought up only to make the point that "opinions differ" and "different views must be respected." When demands for freedom and for tolerance of diversity dominate public discussion, the perception is readily fostered that "one way of looking at things is as good as another," that the adoption of a particular perspective can hardly be a matter of urgency, and that insistence upon language of right and wrong is the hallmark of the narrow-minded.

4. The misgivings about the language of right and wrong noted in the preceding paragraph are the (perhaps unintended) result of relegating—by etiquette no less than by law—religion and moral conviction to private spheres. Yet the worldview of many people today itself leaves little place for such language, at least in its traditional usage. Where nature is thought to show only mechanical order, morality may be dismissed as the mere convention of society or as the invention of one class of people to promote its interests by controlling the conduct of others. Viewed more positively, the moral sense of humans may be thought of as an asset acquired in the process of human evolution, serving to promote human survival and well-being. Alternatively, conventions of morality may be regarded as the product of human culture honed over millennia into a fairly dependable guide to the individual's welfare in society. Still, even these more favorable understandings of morality convey, at best, a reason for thinking it prudent or beneficial (in some respect) to follow morality's

dictates. It is not clear why one is *right* to conform either to a useful convention or to an evolutionary development within our species, or in what sense one would be *wrong* if one refused to do so. On any of these current views, the terms have lost much of their traditional force.

5. Finally, moderns know that heredity and environment greatly affect human attitudes and actions. Even when we cannot avoid looking upon certain kinds of conduct with disapproval, we readily agree to the reminder that a number of factors for which the culprits in question bear no responsibility have contributed to (if not determined) their behavior. Is it appropriate, then, to use the language of right and wrong, with its connotations of "praiseworthy" and "blameworthy"?

And yet, for all of our misgivings, we have not dispensed with the language of right and wrong—and, in the end, we would not want to do so. Most of us, if pressed, would insist that Hitler, or Stalin, or the classroom bully of our primary school days, made a fair number of choices that were not merely imprudent, unwise, or nonbeneficial, but—in some fundamental, not merely conventional sense—*wrong*. Teachers today usually insist that they are not imposing *their* moral standards on students. But if Johnny persists in seeing nothing amiss in cheating, or in shutting up cats inside automatic dryers and turning on the machines, many of us would hope that his teacher will succeed in introducing Johnny to some (rather traditional) notions of moral behavior. For all our awareness of the impact of heredity and environment, our legal systems continue to assume that we should hold most people responsible for most of what they do; so, too, does our everyday conversation. And for all our assurance that we can account for human moral sentiments by means of some such explanation as those given above, we still find that the explanations fail to yield satisfactory answers to moral dilemmas that persist in arising. "How much attention *ought* I to give a senile parent, or a handicapped child?" The question may not occur to people naturally kind or notoriously self-absorbed. But it occurs to others and is likely to remain an issue, urgent and unresolved,

> For all of our misgivings, we have not dispensed with the language of right and wrong—and, in the end, we would not want to do so.

even if we convince ourselves that the sentiments urging us to act are the product of a quirk of evolution or of arbitrary human convention.

Enough has been said of the modern ambivalence toward the language of right and wrong to provide a background against which we may explore the quite different thinking of the apostle Paul. The task of seeing sin through his eyes must surely rank among our most formidable undertakings. Nor will definitions, however precise, even begin to evoke for contemporary readers Paul's sense of sin. Narrative (in this case, a series of short narratives) provides (again) our best starting point.

An Approach to "Sin"

First, then, a series of related parables.[2]

1. Ashley and Chrystal, exchange students in Paris, spend thirty-two and a half minutes in the halls of the Louvre, chatting and giggling all the while about the boys they left behind them. They later report that the museum had a lot of paintings.

2. Brandon enters his brother's room, sees it transformed into a boyish fort, stifles the thought that his own room is not nearly as neat, and trashes in seconds what his brother had spent hours in constructing. Called to account for his action, Brandon asks how he was supposed to know that the stupid mop was supposed to be a stupid flag, that the stupid pile of books was a stupid tower, that the stupid sticks were stupid soldiers. No one had told *him*. He was, most unfairly (he felt), sent to his room.

3. Ashley and Chrystal, upon entering a cathedral of staggering beauty, spend six and three-quarter minutes telling jokes as they aimlessly wander the aisles. Outside one of its chapels, attendants request them either to be a little quieter or to talk outside, since a funeral is in progress. They leave in a huff. Asked later what they had seen that day, they forget to mention Notre Dame.

2. Verisimilitude, it should be remembered, is not essential to the genre. Caricature—introduced to make a point—is quite in order. Resemblances between the figures of my parables and real live people of my own or the reader's acquaintance are strictly coincidental.

4. Like many boys, Brandon likes catching butterflies, frogs, and snakes. Like some boys, Brandon likes cutting them up with his knife.

5. Ashley and Chrystal are taken by their hosts to the Swiss Alps. At the Matterhorn, at Lake Geneva, at countless other sites of breathtaking beauty, the breath of Ashley and Chrystal is devoted to nonstop trivial conversation. To their credit, they do remember later that there are a "whole lot of mountains" in Switzerland, though they are decidedly of the opinion that, if you have seen one mountain, you have seen them all.

6. Brandon, now in his midteens and brandishing a bottle, saunters across a Little League baseball diamond, pretending not to notice that a game is in progress. He kicks second base into right field, makes fun of the "squirt" who retrieves it, showers the left fielder with the remains of his bottle. Challenged to move on, Brandon snorts that *he* always thought it was a free country, that he will leave when he feels like it. The feeling apparently comes over him at the very moment when he sees a police cruiser pass slowly by the field.

7. Ashley and Chrystal return home to New Jersey. At the airport, waiting to see them, are their parents, who had worked long and hard, but proudly, to send their daughters to France. Ashley and Chrystal, engrossed in trivial conversation, initially walk past their parents in the lounge. Hearing their names, they half-turn their heads to inquire, "Where's the car?"

8. At dusk, several hours after the game, Brandon returns to a now-abandoned field and discovers a catcher's mitt that was left behind. It never occurs to Brandon to take the glove; what would *he* do with a catcher's mitt? Instead, he brandishes his penknife and cuts the glove to shreds. He is about to leave the field when he bumps into an anxious father and son running toward the field. Sizing up the situation, Brandon anticipates their outcry with a shrug: "You leave it, you lose it."

9. High school days over, needing something to do, Ashley and Chrystal decide to become social workers. One of their first assignments takes them to assess the needs of a young widow with three small children recently thrust into Ashley and Chrystal's community from a war zone in the third world. Ashley and Chrystal spend fifty-one and a half minutes of their one-hour

visit in wide-ranging chatter with each other. They later report that the refugees will probably need food.

10. Several years later, again at dusk, Brandon comes upon a little girl playing by herself in a park near some trees. "Shouldn't have left her alone," he mutters.

In at least the later stories, readers will agree, something is not quite (or not at all) as it should be. The *root* of our feeling is scarcely some sense that people are breaking laws; apart from, presumably, the tenth episode and, possibly, the sixth, the law is not even an issue. Nor would most of us readily think of moral rules that have been infringed. In some cases we could come up with a rule that, if it had been kept, would have led Ashley, Brandon, or Chrystal (hereafter ABC) to behave differently. Had, for example, AC been reminded of some such principle as "Gratitude should be shown toward benefactors" (or even "Honor your father and your mother"), they might not have shown the thoughtlessness of episode 7. But for most of us, such a rule would represent a secondary attempt to articulate and to generalize a more spontaneous feeling about what is proper in a situation like that in the episode. The rule, however serviceable, is not the *source* of our moral sentiment.

On the other hand, to the extent that we are prepared to insist that our moral sentiments in these cases are warranted, we *are* saying that the scope of behavior allowed by human freedom is much wider than the range of actions that we deem appropriate. AC may be *free* to ignore their parents; but they are inconsiderate if they do so. And could they not have responded more sympathetically to the widow in episode 9? Perhaps B is *free* to cut to shreds a catcher's mitt that he finds; but he *must* have been aware that the mitt meant a lot to someone and that his act of destruction served no good purpose. And—forgetting the illegality—how *could* he treat the innocence, or the very life, of a child as having no value beyond the gratification of a moment's destructive urge?

> The scope of behavior allowed by human freedom is much wider than the range of actions that we deem appropriate. Self-absorbed people need to open their eyes to the reality of a world much bigger than themselves.

Common to each of the episodes is the self-absorption of ABC. B's self-preoccupation is pernicious in ways that AC's is not. Still, when confronted with some reality not of their own making, they all proceed at least to ignore it, at worst to belittle it, trample on it, abuse it. Little League games and cathedrals, a boyish fort and the Matterhorn, butterflies, parents, a child at play, and a widow: these realities external to ABC elicit from them either no response whatever (in AC's case) or (in B's) a perverse insistence on his freedom to do as he pleases. AC, we may feel, need to grow up; B needs to change his ways. All three need to open their eyes to the reality of a world much bigger than themselves.

"Sin" in Proverbs

The book of Proverbs is replete with expressions of moral sentiment. Yet those sentiments are seldom related to any code of moral law; in that respect they are like our own. And a premise underlying the argument of the whole book is that humans have wide powers to do as they choose: in an important sense they are (as we like to emphasize) *free*. But the argument that Proverbs builds on that premise is that some of our potential choices are appropriate, right, and wise, while others are inappropriate and disastrous. We did not make the world; we are constantly confronted with realities not of our choosing or design; and how we respond to these realities betrays our character and ultimately—the world being what it is—determines our fate.

Much of Proverbs is made up, not of direct moral counsel, but simply of observations and reminders that in the world as we know it, certain kinds of behavior entail certain predictable consequences. The point, whether implicit or explicit, is that the wise bear this in mind, while the foolish, by definition, do not. Providing security for the loans of people you hardly know is not a wise thing to do.[3] Inactivity at seedtime and harvest invites disaster (even the ants know better!).[4] So does a refusal to listen to the advice of others.[5] So do a quick temper, a loose tongue,

3. Proverbs 11:15.
4. Proverbs 6:6–11; 20:4.
5. Proverbs 12:1; 15:32.

pride and excessive self-assurance, addiction to strong drink, and, indeed, the consumption of too much honey.[6] Of course, humans are *free* in all these matters to ignore what experience has long since discovered about the nature of reality. If they do, however, they will pay the price.

In the instances given above, the cause-and-effect pattern is no doubt apparent even today. But the list in Proverbs goes on. Wrong, wicked, foolish, and baneful behavior includes slander and gossip, cheating in business, accepting bribes, charging exorbitant interest, adultery, cruelty to animals, turning a deaf ear to the cries of the needy.[7] For Proverbs, the point is the same in these cases as in the preceding. We do not live in an unstructured, value-neutral world where we are free to decide what is best for ourselves. The world—by divine wisdom—has been given an order that is good, promoting our life and well-being. Human freedom (Proverbs itself does not use the term) amounts to the power people have to choose

> A slack hand causes poverty,
>   but the hand of the diligent
>   makes rich.
> Hatred stirs up strife,
>   but love covers all offenses.
> Whoever heeds instruction is on
>   the path to life,
>   but one who rejects a rebuke
>   goes astray.
> When words are many,
>   transgression is not lacking,
>   but the prudent are restrained
>   in speech.
> Like vinegar to the teeth, and
>   smoke to the eyes,
>   so are the lazy to their
>   employers.
>
> Proverbs 10:4,
> 12, 17, 19, 26 NRSV

their response to the divinely created order. We can respect and celebrate and live in harmony with it by being honest in speech, fair and compassionate in our dealings with others, diligent in doing what needs to be done, reverent toward God: a course of life that is "righteous" and "wise" and conducive to our own good. Or we can refuse to recognize any good that we ourselves do not define and that does not have us as its focus—thus defying the order in which we cannot help but live. Proverbs' phrase for those who make such a choice is that they

6. Proverbs 14:17; 13:3; 11:2; 28:26; 20:1; 25:16.
7. Proverbs 10:18; 11:13; 11:1; 17:23; 28:8; 6:24–35; 12:10; 21:13.

are "wise in [their] own eyes."[8] Their path, the book insists, can only end in disaster. Proverbs uses all the resources at its disposal to encourage people to choose the good.

Three further features of the argument of Proverbs merit brief mention here.

1. Proverbs frequently speaks as though the moral order itself

> Wisdom cries out in the street;
>   in the squares she raises her voice. . . .
> "How long, O simple ones, will you love being simple?
> How long will scoffers delight in their scoffing
>   and fools hate knowledge?
> Give heed to my reproof;
> I will pour out my thoughts to you;
>   I will make my words known to you.
> Because I have called and you refused,
>   have stretched out my hand and no one heeded,
> and because you have ignored all my counsel
>   and would have none of my reproof,
> I also will laugh at your calamity;
>   I will mock when panic strikes you. . . .
> Because they hated knowledge
>   and did not choose the fear of the LORD,
> would have none of my counsel,
>   and despised all my reproof,
> therefore they shall eat the fruit of their way
>   and be sated with their own devices. . . .
> But those who listen to me will be secure
>   and will live at ease, without dread of disaster."
>
> Proverbs 1:20–33 NRSV

recoils and brings disaster upon those who flout and abuse it. Such people will eat the fruit of their own way; their perversity will be their own death.[9] Other texts, however, speak of God as overseeing and enforcing the moral order: the good obtain favor

8. Proverbs 3:7.
9. See, for example, Proverbs 1:31–32.

from him, whereas he condemns those who concoct evil.[10] The two perspectives are quite compatible: the moral order, put in place and supervised by a righteous God, perfectly expresses his love of righteousness and hatred of evil by promoting the well-being of the righteous and assuring the calamitous end of the wicked.

2. In such a world, taking God into account (literally, "fearing" him) is the first and most essential step in coming to terms with reality.[11] If God is the Maker of all and human destiny is in his hands, then it does indeed follow that our most appropriate and urgent response to the reality that confronts us is to give God his due.

3. Proverbs repeatedly speaks as though material prosperity inevitably follows wise and righteous living, whereas earthly calamity accompanies the path of wickedness. From the perspective of other biblical traditions and later Jewish and Christian thought, that notion is too simplistic. The point of Proverbs—that we find ourselves confronted with a reality and an order not of our making, and that we may respond in appropriate or inappropriate ways—is central to Jewish and Christian visions of reality. That our choices, frequently enough, bear fit and immediate consequences is also a common insistence. But we need only cite the book of Job in the Hebrew Scriptures and the Beatitudes in the Christian[12] to remind ourselves that Jews and Christians alike would concede that divine enforcement of the moral order has a rationale and a timetable not transparent to human view.

> The fear of the LORD is the beginning of knowledge;
> fools despise wisdom and instruction.
>
> Proverbs 1:7 NRSV

Nor is Proverbs itself insensitive to this point. Together with texts that relate fearing the Lord to fullness of barns[13] are others that claim that it is "better" to be poor than dishonest, "better" to be upright and poor than crooked and rich.[14] In what sense

10. See Proverbs 12:2.
11. More literally, it is "the beginning of knowledge" (Proverbs 1:7).
12. See Matthew 5:3–12.
13. Proverbs 3:7–10.
14. Proverbs 19:22; 28:6.

better? Proverbs has no vocabulary to develop the point. There is a rightness in God's world. In the end, it is somehow better to live in harmony with that rightness under any conditions than to defy it, for whatever apparent gain.

... and in Paul

Paul's depiction of human sinfulness in Romans 1:18–32 is essentially a restatement of perspectives already apparent in Proverbs. Here we will largely be content to note the parallels.

1. Paul does not refer in this passage to divine law. Human sinfulness here is a matter of willfully inappropriate responses to reality, not the transgression of a specified moral code.

2. If sin is inappropriate response to reality, the fundamental human sin (for Paul as for Proverbs) is the failure to respond appropriately to the Creator of all that is. Those who are in the presence of awesome natural or artistic beauty and yet fail to respond with wonder betray their own self-absorption and insensitivity. Similarly, for Paul, to enjoy life in a world created and ordered by divine goodness without responding with thanks to God is unnatural, perverse, sinful—and the root of all other sins.[15] Other sins represent a refusal to live in harmony with some *aspect* of the divine order of creation. They follow inevitably from a refusal to give recognition to the Creator himself. For Paul, sin at its root is something far more egregious than the violation of rules; it represents the rejecting and insulting of a person—indeed, of the very One to whom humans owe everything they are and have and who himself wills their own well-being.

3. To be properly "sinful," human "sinfulness" must be inexcusable. Paul stresses that humans refuse to acknowledge God despite having the evidence for his power and deity before their eyes, and that people sin in sundry ways in spite of an awareness

> There is a rightness in God's world. In the end, it is better to live in harmony with that rightness under any conditions than to defy it, for whatever apparent gain.

15. Romans 1:19–23, 28.

that envy, murder, strife, deceit, and the like are wrong.[16] Human
sin thus goes beyond the wrongfulness of individual acts to include in each case a suppression of, a willful blindness toward,
the truth of human dependence upon God.[17] We did not make our
world. But when we defy its order
and goodness with our greed,
malice, slander, and faithlessness,
we assume the right of creators
to define the terms of their own
existence. Such is the lie—the "dis-
obeying of the truth"[18]—implicit in
every sin. Paul also claims, however, that such sin affects human
minds. To sin against the light one
has can only lead to the darkening
of one's powers of perception (no
doubt because, in the inevitable
process of justifying their conduct to themselves and others,
sinners skew their own moral and
religious sensibilities).[19] This point
will become important in our next
chapter.

4. Illustrative of the human refusal to acknowledge the created
order are, for Paul, the homosexual activities of both women
and men.[20] Paul knew nothing of modern constructions of such
activities as expressing a genetically determined sexual orientation or even a disorder brought on by a dysfunctional childhood. Others today stress the personal choice involved in such
activity—and in this respect they are closer to Paul. In Paul's
perception and experience, homosexual activity represented an
outlet for sexual energies chosen by people who paid no heed to

> For the wrath of God is revealed from heaven against all ungodliness and wickedness of those who by their wickedness suppress the truth. For what can be known about God is plain to them, because God has shown it to them. Ever since the creation of the world his eternal power and divine nature, invisible though they are, have been understood and seen through the things he has made. So they are without excuse; for though they knew God, they did not honor him as God or give thanks to him. . . . They did not see fit to acknowledge God.
>
> Romans 1:18–21, 28 NRSV

16. Romans 1:18–21, 29–32.
17. Romans 1:18, 28.
18. Romans 2:8.
19. See Romans 1:21–22.
20. Romans 1:26–27.

the appropriate place of sexuality in the created order. For Paul, sexual activity was fitting within marriage;[21] indeed, he saw the natural desire of one sex for union with the other as properly attracting them to marry.[22] On this score Paul was merely articulating in his day the divine sanction given to marriage in the Hebrew Scriptures: God created humanity as "male and female," intending, for their own well-being, that a man and a woman should become "one flesh," thus providing companionship for each other and offspring to "fill the earth."[23] Hence, Paul maintains, to indulge sexual passion outside of marriage, or with another's spouse, is sin.[24] One is, in effect, seizing the goods of the created order on one's own terms, without the attendant commitment and responsibilities. The distortion is particularly self-evident when sexual gratification is sought with members of one's own sex.[25]

> Therefore God gave them up in the lusts of their hearts to impurity. . . . For this reason God gave them up to degrading passions. . . . Since they did not see fit to acknowledge God, God gave them up to a debased mind and to things that should not be done.
>
> Romans 1:24, 26, 28 NRSV

5. The very being of God responds with abhorrence to the defiance and defilement of creation's goodness: on this point the Hebrew Scriptures are united. Paul reasserts the claim with his reference to divine "wrath" against all human "ungodliness" and "wickedness" in Romans 1:18. The divine way of dealing with human sin, as Paul describes it in Romans 1:24–31, appears to be a variant of the traditional view (amply attested in Proverbs)

21. Note the contrast in 1 Thessalonians 4:3–4 between fornication and the "holiness" and "honor" of sexual intercourse within marriage. See also 1 Corinthians 7:3–4.

22. First Corinthians 7:2, 9, 36. The whole passage asserts, however, Paul's conviction that exceptional circumstances should lead at least some people to adopt other priorities.

23. Genesis 1:27–28; 2:18, 24.

24. See 1 Corinthians 6:9–10, 18.

25. Note Paul's emphasis on the un*naturalness* (the opposition to the design of nature) involved when men abandon intercourse "with women" for relations of "men . . . with men" (Romans 1:27). The terminology rules out the suggestion that Paul faults only exploitative relationships involving males of different social statuses. See also Leviticus 18:22.

that the created order recoils and wreaks havoc upon those who defy it. God, Paul states, has "given up," or "abandoned," sinners to the degradation of their own sins. Those who refuse to respect and comply with the goodness of creation must live in a world marred by their own envy, murder, strife, faithlessness, heartlessness, ruthlessness. Present conditions, in Paul's eyes, are thus themselves in some measure a revelation of God's wrath—though Paul will also insist on a coming, decisive judgment.[26]

In this passage Paul does not discuss natural evil: disease, destructive storms, earthquakes, and the like.[27] Nor, indeed, does natural evil frequently appear as a problem in the corpus of the Hebrew Scriptures. Paul's attention is focused rather on the *moral* evil—the "*un*righteousness"—of human beings. In claiming that such evil represents a perverse and inexcusable response to the goodness of God and of the created order, Paul implies and reasserts fundamental tenets of the "Jewish-Christian" worldview. Among the creatures on God's earth, humans are distinct in their capacity for making moral choices. Yet we have all done things that, we well know, we ought not to have done. In the process we have sullied the innocence both of ourselves and of our world. To be sure, we choose our own actions. But we do so in a world in which there are appropriate responses to the reality that confronts us, and other responses that are inappropriate. There is right and there is wrong, there is good and there is evil. And which we do makes a profound difference.

26. Romans 2:5–11, 16.
27. He does, however, reflect on such evil in Romans 8:19–23.

4

Israel Joins the Fray

Romans 2:1–3:20

In our day, sentences beginning "Thou shalt not" are liable to lose their audience before they reach their end. Those who insist on freedom to define what is good for themselves tend to resent prohibitions like those of the Ten Commandments[1] as unwarranted attempts to limit their options. Clearly, we need to broaden our horizons if we are to see the law of Moses through the eyes of a Paul. In this chapter we consider a few aspects of the propriety of law in the "Jewish-Christian" worldview,[2] proceed by noting the centrality of "torah" in the book of Deuteronomy, then conclude with a comparison of Deuteronomy's perspective with Paul's discussion of Jews and their laws in Romans 2:1–3:20.

---

1. Exodus 20:1–17; Deuteronomy 5:6–21. Paul's understanding of the Mosaic law will be treated in more detail in chapter 9, below.
2. For the sense in which I use the phrase, see chapter 1, note 7.

The Place of Moral Law

In the preceding chapter, examples from the lives of Ashley, Brandon, and Chrystal illustrated (1) that not all that humans are "free" to do represents appropriate behavior on their part (Ashley and Chrystal, you may recall, acted quite thoughtlessly toward their parents and a widow in need); (2) that the *root* of

---

The Ten Commandments (the Decalogue)

I am the LORD your God, who brought you out of the land of Egypt, out of the house of slavery; you shall have no other gods before me.

You shall not make for yourself an idol, whether in the form of anything that is in heaven above, or that is on the earth beneath, or that is in the water under the earth. You shall not bow down to them or worship them . . .

You shall not make wrongful use of the name of the LORD your God; for the LORD will not acquit anyone who misuses his name.

Remember the sabbath day, and keep it holy. Six days you shall labor and do all your work. But the seventh day is a sabbath to the LORD your God; you shall not do any work . . .

Honor your father and your mother, so that your days may be long in the land that the LORD your God is giving you.

You shall not murder.

You shall not commit adultery.

You shall not steal.

You shall not bear false witness against your neighbor.

You shall not covet . . . anything that belongs to your neighbor.

Exodus 20:2–17 NRSV

---

our sense that some actions are *not* appropriate is not a belief that laws have been broken (we are not likely to think of laws when we assess Ashley and Chrystal's behavior); and (3) that we can nonetheless *think* of laws (such as "Gratitude should be shown toward benefactors," or "Honor your father and your mother") that, if observed, would keep people from behaving in the inappropriate ways of Ashley and Chrystal.

Along similar lines we can grasp the place of divine law in the "Jewish-Christian" worldview. Inherent in such a view is the conviction that the goodness of God elicits both appropriate and inappropriate (or sinful) responses from his creatures. Laws are not needed for behavior to be found inappropriate; yet laws *can* be formulated that spell out—and, if observed, prevent—such behavior. If life and love, health and sustenance are all gifts from the hands of God, then wholehearted devotion to him is only fitting: the law rightly requires such devotion.[3] Conversely, to withhold worship from God, or to give to any other the reverence, love, and trust that are properly the Lord's, would be perverse: the law rightly condemns such conduct.[4] An appropriate response to reality can hardly take the form of misrepresenting the actions of others[5] or of taking—or even desiring—for oneself what others' work has made their own.[6] Respect for life as a gift from God to others as well as to oneself will make the thought of murder abhorrent.[7] In each of these cases, the law can be seen to spell out what behavior is appropriate, and what inappropriate, for humans in God's world.

Marriage, moreover, in the biblical tradition, is no mere agreement between two people to live together as long as they both so choose, but itself an institution of divine creation, a project greater than themselves, in which a man and a woman may nonetheless be enlisted. Since it is God who made man and woman such that they are attracted to each other, God who designed that in this way they could draw strength from their mutual companionship, and God who ordained that their relationship should provide a fit setting for the birth and care of children, marriage is to be sanctified and celebrated as a gift to human well-being from

3. "You shall love the LORD your God with all your heart, and with all your soul, and with all your might" (Deuteronomy 6:5 NRSV).

4. "You shall have no other gods before me" (Exodus 20:3 NRSV).

5. "You shall not bear false witness against your neighbor" (Exodus 20:16 NRSV). The commandment was intended to exclude false witness in a legal setting. Still, slander and deception of any kind were subject to censure (see, for example, Proverbs 10:18; 12:22), and the prohibition of "false witness" was easily interpreted as forbidding all lying.

6. "You shall not steal" (Exodus 20:15 NRSV). "You shall not covet" (Exodus 20:17 NRSV).

7. "You shall not murder" (Exodus 20:13 NRSV). See also Genesis 9:5–6.

a benevolent Creator.[8] The joys of sexual intimacy—as husband and wife become "one flesh"—are among its obvious enticements and rewards.[9] From this perspective, then, those who engage in the procreative act outside of such a relationship are involved in deceit, either by pretending to express a committed love to which they have not bound themselves (perhaps even acting in defiance of a relationship to which they *have* bound themselves), or by simply disregarding the created order and trivializing its gift of

---

In the biblical view, humans flourish as they submit to God's laws. Psalm 19 expresses this understanding marvelously:

The law of the LORD is perfect, reviving the soul;

  the decrees of the LORD are sure, making wise the simple;

  the precepts of the LORD are right, rejoicing the heart;

  the commandment of the LORD is clear, enlightening the eyes;

  the fear of the LORD is pure, enduring forever;

  the ordinances of the LORD are true and righteous altogether.

More to be desired are they than gold, even much fine gold;

  sweeter also than honey, and drippings of the honeycomb.

Moreover by them is your servant warned;

  in keeping them there is great reward.

Psalm 19:7–11 NRSV

---

sexuality. Hence, the prohibition of "adultery."[10] Furthermore, that children should honor those to whom they owe birth and breeding represents both the fulfillment of a natural obligation

---

8. Genesis 1:27–28; 2:18–25; Proverbs 18:22; 19:14; Matthew 19:4–6.

9. Genesis 2:24; Proverbs 5:15–20.

10. Exodus 20:14. Note also the esteem accorded marriage, and the warning against its violation, in Hebrews 13:4; and see 1 Thessalonians 4:3–4. The commandment forbidding "adultery" literally prohibits a man from engaging in sexual relations with another's wife. The Mosaic law judged differently the intercourse of a man (even a married man) with an unmarried (and unengaged) woman, and a number of narratives of the Hebrew Bible suggest that such acts were not subject to significant public censure. The New Testament writings are, however, uniform in their condemnation of intercourse outside of marriage, and moral thinkers came to see such a condemnation as implicit in the creation texts of Genesis.

and the cultivation of a proper reverence for the created order within which they must live.[11]

Such laws, within the context of the "Jewish-Christian" worldview, are not unwarranted commands curtailing human freedom any more than are the physical demands that people eat, drink, breathe, and sleep. Just as the human body requires sustenance and repose to prosper, so the human spirit is seen as having a capacity for communion with the Eternal, for zeal for truth, and for giving itself in love. Humans flourish only when these aspects of their nature are given due expression. As long as our human will (by which we choose what we do) is united with our reason and we cherish what we deem to be true and good, we feel no constraint when we respond to these demands of reality upon us. They become a constraint only when we assign more importance to doing what we *choose* than to doing what is appropriate and right. For such a will, bent on its own self-assertion, on declaring its independence from the created order, the demands of reality are inevitably experienced as constrictive. But the laws of creation are unwelcome only to those who choose to live in defiance of reality and who are thus, necessarily, at odds with the conditions of their own well-being.

A further conviction, however, also central to the "Jewish-Christian" view, is that such an alienation has affected all of humankind. Paul's depiction of humanity's bondage to sin is more radical than a number of other perspectives, particularly within Judaism. But the hearts of men and women are everywhere seen as having an inclination toward evil from their youth;[12] and the story of Adam and Eve,[13] though subject to different interpretations, means nothing if not that humanity suffers the bane that follows from human self-assertion.

Inevitably, humans who exercise their will in opposition to their perception of what is right attempt to patch together their now-divided personality. Human reason must justify what the human will has chosen, even at the cost of falsifying reality. The "Jewish-Christian" view insists that choices between good and evil must be made. Yet it is in principle open to the notion that

11. Exodus 20:12.
12. Genesis 8:21; 6:5.
13. Genesis 2–3.

the moral codes actually current in human society present the boundary between evil and good in a distorted form. Not only are such codes culturally influenced;[14] they are often blind to, or even supportive of, injustice and oppression. Such limitations are only to be expected: moral codes, after all, are formulated and passed on by human beings. The terms of the codes come to reflect not only people's tugging awareness of the obligation to do the right, but also their determination to do as they choose—and their need to legitimate their choices in terms of their (now perverted) moral sensibilities.

The Place of Law in Deuteronomy

The "Jewish-Christian" vision can account for the plurality of human moral codes and for the distorted perceptions they contain. A good God, however, can hardly be content to leave human beings in doubt, however self-induced, about what is right and life-promoting for them to do. The central theme of the book of Deuteronomy is that God chose to spell out the path of life for a people whose attention and indebtedness he had already secured by mighty acts of divine redemption. Thus, to Israel, delivered from bondage in Egypt, God revealed his *torah*.

A number of torah's demands merely state what must be the appropriate responses that humans of any age or place should make to the reality defined by the "Jewish-Christian" worldview; the "righteousness" of such laws, Deuteronomy believes, is self-evident to all.[15] Some demands in Deuteronomy, as Jews and Christians both concede, while expressing principles fundamental to the human condition, adapt those principles to the peculiar circumstances prevailing among those to whom torah was first given.[16] Still other demands are in themselves arbitrary;[17] the

14. The fundamental demands of morality take somewhat different forms in different cultures.

15. Deuteronomy 4:5–8.

16. Some of these, indeed, now seem oppressive. Note, for example, that the conditions of slaves are presupposed, though ameliorated, by the provisions of Deuteronomy 15:12–18.

17. So at least some representatives of the Jewish tradition have emphasized. With them we may reckon Paul. The argument of Romans 14 assumes that there is no inherent reason why certain foods should be forbidden or certain days (and

text gives no rationale, for example, for the commanded exclusion of certain foods from Israelite diets.[18] Both the imposition of arbitrary divine demands and Israel's submission to them are justified, however, as fitting exhibits of the relationship between God and his people: even in deciding what food they should eat, God's people are not to pursue an independent path, but to delight in submission to the will of their benevolent Lord.

Jews use the term *torah* for divine guidance, however it is given. A more technical usage employs *Torah* to name the opening five books of the Hebrew Scriptures (the "books of Moses"). In Deuteronomy, torah refers to the divine stipulations that the people of Israel undertook to observe when they entered a "covenant" with God. No peculiar goodness on Israel's part moved God to distinguish them with his favor.[19] But love them he did, and to make them "his" people, he liberated them from slavery to Pharaoh,[20] brought them "on eagles' wings" to Mount Sinai, and gave them laws by which they could demonstrate their loyalty to his rule. As they do so, Deuteronomy never tires of intoning, they will prosper. Should they fail to do so, Deuteronomy never wearies of warning, they will perish. The choice is one of blessing or cursing, life or death.[21]

> See, just as the Lord my God has charged me [Moses], I now teach you statutes and ordinances for you to observe in the land that you are about to enter and occupy. You must observe them diligently, for this will show your wisdom and discernment to the peoples, who, when they hear all these statutes, will say, "Surely this great nation is a wise and discerning people!" For what other great nation . . . has statutes and ordinances as just as this entire law that I am setting before you today?
>
> Deuteronomy 4:5–8 NRSV

In a number of ways, Deuteronomy's view of God's covenant with Israel provides a model of what, in the "Jewish-Christian" view, should be the relationship between God and his human

---

not others) observed as holy; yet Paul acknowledges that such observances can be a legitimate way to serve God.

18. Deuteronomy 14:3–21.
19. Deuteronomy 7:6–8; 9:4–6.
20. The story is told in Exodus 1–15.
21. Deuteronomy 11:26–28; 30:15–20.

creatures of all nations. Jews are thus meant to serve as a
"light" to the peoples of the world.[22] God, as the source of good
for all humankind, is the proper and worthy object of human
devotion and trust. Israel's—and all humanity's—obedience
is fitting, not only because the Creator enjoys the prerogative
to command his creatures, but also because his requirements
spell out the terms of their own well-being. But divine demands
compel human decisions. It is not for humans to *decide* what
is good, thus imposing their own order and value on the world
in which they live. In Deuteronomy, the good confronts Israel
in the divine commands of torah. For all humanity, in the
"Jewish-Christian" view, the nature of the good is given in the
already-structured, already-valued world of divine creation.
The choice—for Israel and for all human beings—is whether
people will *do* the good, thus aligning themselves with reality, or flout the good and live a lie, to their own inevitable
destruction.

Deuteronomy stresses the starkness of the choice. God's demands, it insists, are neither complex nor difficult.[23] Yet Israel,
the book repeatedly decries, seems constitutionally incapable
of complying. This theme reaches its climax in chapter 32, the
Song of Moses. God's people are "perverse and crooked," "foolish
and senseless."[24] They respond to God's goodness with a mulish
and mutinous kick.[25] The chapter anticipates the detailing of
Israel's recalcitrance in the books of Joshua, Judges, Samuel,
and Kings, a story ending in divine judgment and exile.[26] Hope
remains, however: if only Israel repents and returns to the Lord,
he remains willing to deal mercifully with his people.[27] But for
that to happen, Deuteronomy proposes, the divine Surgeon will
need to "circumcise" Israel's "heart," cutting away its ingrained
perversity.[28]

22. For the notion, see Isaiah 43:10; 45:14; 60:2–3.
23. Deuteronomy 10:12–13; 30:11–14.
24. Deuteronomy 32:5–6, 28.
25. Deuteronomy 32:15–18.
26. For other traditional statements of Israel's intractability, see Psalms 78
and 106, Ezekiel 20, and Nehemiah 9.
27. Deuteronomy 4:25–31; 30:1–5.
28. Deuteronomy 30:6.

. . . and in Paul

In the latter half of Romans 1, Paul denounced, without referring to divine law, the human revolt against reality: humans refuse to acknowledge God, defy the moral order of creation, engage in and even "applaud" activities they know to be wrong. That humans have moral sensibilities is presupposed in the observation that they defy them.

Throughout chapter 2, a close relationship between human moral sensibilities and the Mosaic law is either stated or implied.[29] When Gentiles do what is right, they show (Paul believes) that, though they have no scroll of the law of God, its demand is "written on their hearts" and has left its imprint on their "conscience."[30] Both Gentiles and Jews are to be judged according to their works: well-doing will be rewarded, wickedness punished.[31] Paul insists on such judgment without any suggestion that good and evil have different content for Jews and Gentiles, though for the former, but not the latter, the terms are spelled out in the Mosaic code. Later in the letter, Paul claims that the commands of the law are "holy and just and good."[32] As in Deuteronomy 4:8, the point must be that what the Mosaic law demands of its subjects is no different from what the conditions of life in God's world demand of all human beings, Jews and Gentiles alike.[33]

Like Deuteronomy, Paul sees the Mosaic law as a gift of God's goodness to the Jews. The willful resistance of human beings to the demands of the truth has left them "blind," "in darkness," "foolish," and in need of instruction. Guidance has been provided for Jews by the gift of torah,[34] a gift that enables them to enlighten others.[35]

29. References to "law" in this section of Romans usually refer to the Mosaic code; the metaphorical usage in Romans 2:14 is an obvious exception.
30. Romans 2:14–15.
31. Romans 2:6–11.
32. Romans 7:12.
33. In these texts Paul ignores the more arbitrary demands of the law (the food laws, for example) traditionally seen as binding only on Jews and enabling them further to express their adherence to the divine will.
34. The law is thus the "embodiment of knowledge and truth" (Romans 2:20 NRSV).
35. Romans 2:17–20.

Do they, however, first teach themselves?[36] After all, hearing the law is not the same as obeying it, and God can approve only the latter.[37] As in Deuteronomy, Israel's encounter with the divine demand compels a human decision; and Paul, like Deuteronomy 32 (a chapter he frequently cites) and the Deuteronomistic History of Joshua–2 Kings, believes that Israel's recalcitrance is inveterate. It was right for God to remind his rebellious creatures of the demands of life in his world. It was, moreover, a great gift to the people of Israel when they were entrusted with the guidance of torah's commands. But the response of human beings to divine law, in whatever form they encounter it, proves the same: they assert their independence by doing what is wrong. God's gift of the law has done nothing to alter this fundamental bent of the human will. The law's practical effect has been to indict, not remedy, human sinfulness.[38]

> Now we know that whatever the law says, it speaks to those who are under the law, so that every mouth may be silenced, and the whole world may be held accountable to God. For "no human being will be justified in his sight" by deeds prescribed by the law, for through the law comes the knowledge of sin.
>
> Romans 3:19–20 NRSV

In conclusion, we note three features of Paul's argument.

1. Paul allows that human beings (even Gentiles!) may do good,[39] yet he declares all humankind to be culpable before God.[40] His point is not that no one ever does things that are right, but rather that all people do things that are wrong. Indeed, the very selectivity with which humans sometimes choose to do the right, sometimes the wrong, may itself be seen as an expression of their setting themselves up as moral arbiters independent of God.[41]

2. Deuteronomy, like Proverbs, sees humans as experiencing the consequences of their choices during their lives on earth. Paul, in company with most Jews of his day, saw the effects of human deeds extending into the world to come. Such an exten-

---

36. Romans 2:21–24.
37. Romans 2:13.
38. Romans 3:19–20.
39. Romans 2:7, 10, 14, and elsewhere.
40. Romans 3:19–20.
41. We return to this issue in chapter 8, below.

sion might seem to be demanded when the righteous appear to suffer and the wicked to prosper throughout their earthly sojourn: only in the afterlife can due recompense be given.[42] But the extension was also thought to be implicit in the commitment of an eternal God to a relationship with mortal human beings. The language of the Psalms at times invites the interpretation that death itself cannot end the human experience of joy in God's presence.[43] And surely (Jesus reasons in the Gospels), when God identified himself for Moses as the "God of Abraham, Isaac, and Jacob," he was not claiming to be the God of dead people: the relationship of an eternal God with those to whom he is committed must continue beyond their deaths.[44] But the extension of humanity's encounter with the Eternal into the "age to come" inevitably raises the stakes inherent in their choices in *this* life between good and evil, right and wrong, life and death.[45]

3. The Hebrew Scriptures constantly condemn Israel's waywardness, but they also summon Israel to repent. Does Paul not think that Israel *can* repent and do what is right? The answer, as later chapters in Romans clearly show, is no. Deuteronomy itself suggests that God would first need to "circumcise" Israel's heart.[46] Jeremiah, too, speaks of the need for God to change the heart of his people if they are to obey his commands.[47] And Ezekiel proposes a heart transplant as the necessary precondition.[48] Paul's point (developed in later chapters) is similar. Human "flesh" refuses to bow itself to the divine will. To enlist humans on the side of the good, God must first transform humanity.

42. See Daniel 12:2.
43. Psalm 16:9–11; 73:23–26.
44. Matthew 22:31–32. Such is the inner logic with which Jews assimilated belief in life after death—whatever the source of the belief. The latter issue cannot be pursued here.
45. Romans 2:7–10.
46. Deuteronomy 30:6.
47. Jeremiah 31:33.
48. Ezekiel 36:26–27.

5

The Divine Counter

Romans 3:21–31

Some people suffer severe pangs of guilt though they have incurred none; others incur monstrous guilt but betray no signs of disturbance. Why, and why not?

Consider (briefly—there are no profundities here) the following cases.

1. Those of us who have parked cars on side streets without noticing a **NO PARKING** sign are not inclined to feel any guilt about our action. Yet we pay a fine.

2. John feels guilty that he cheated his longtime friend and business partner. He is also, and not coincidentally, liable to prosecution.

3. Jim feels guilty for consuming, in a moment of weakness, food that he has been told he should not eat. The food is in fact harmless to his health.

4. June is distressed, believing that she has been a poor parent. Observers agree that she has done everything for her child that a parent can do.

These cases illustrate the following elementary distinction.

1. We *incur* guilt, whatever our feelings, when we violate a law or norm to which we are subject, as in cases 1 and 2, above.

2. We *feel* guilt when we believe that we have violated a law, norm, or expectation that we believe to be both legitimate and significant, as in cases 2–4. Only in the second example above do incurred guilt and feelings of guilt overlap.

Many people today feel the same ambivalence about guilt as they do about notions of wrongdoing. We can agree on the actual, objective guilt of those who break the laws of society or the rules of some institution or organization of which they are a part. But many are wary of limiting the freedom of individuals by suggesting that there are other—*moral*—norms by which people ought to govern their lives. Some, indeed, insist that there are no such norms, only customs and conventions of particular societies. Others suspect that that goes too far, though they themselves would be unable to articulate or justify a belief in absolute moral standards. Because we refuse to allow universal norms or are unable to defend them, we are left uncertain when, if ever, we have done what we should not; and the pangs of guilt we feel for our doubtful wrongs seem misplaced if not pathological.

Indeed, when the laws of society are no longer thought to reflect *higher* laws of some sort, then it is hard to see why we *ought* to obey them. Clearly, lawbreakers are guilty in a technical, objective sense. But if the laws in force are understood merely as rules concocted to protect the interests and smooth the functioning of society, and if, in other areas, we lionize individual freedom, then we should not be surprised when independently minded individuals wonder why they need to submit to the conventions we call laws, and feel no guilt when they flout them. Who *says*, after all, that the law should not be broken? Society? Why should anyone listen to society? Because it has the power to punish? What if I believe I can escape punishment? Without other resources to supplement it, the rhetoric of individual freedom seems incapable of devising an answer.

Yet many of us are distressed by the brazen absence of any sense of guilt shown by some who commit heinous crimes. We are appalled when people who cheat and swindle, who grossly neglect or abuse their dependents, who murder for the pocket change of their victims, appear to regret only that they were caught. They ought to show some remorse, we protest—though our uncertainty about the status or force of moral claims leaves us ill-equipped to justify the burden of guilt we sense should be theirs.

Such a dilemma is surely a characteristic product of the perspectives and peculiar emphases of contemporary Western society. Paul would have been as hard pressed to see the point of our dilemma as we are to understand his language of atonement. In this chapter we begin with a modern approximation of biblical notions of guilt and atonement, proceed with a few features of their occurrence in the Hebrew Scriptures, then conclude with a few observations on Paul.

Of Guilt and Atonement

Guilt follows from the violation of valid norms. And one norm whose validity most of us would recognize requires that those who benefit from the kindness of others respond with some gesture of reciprocation. "You could at least have said thank you!" is a reproach that we often think justified, though significant benefits, bestowed at considerable sacrifice on the part of the donor, may well require more of us than a mere expression of thanks. Those who accept benefits at others' expense but who withhold any gesture of reciprocation seem to have incurred an outstanding debt. To take a different tack, the positive harm we admittedly do to others would seem to bring us guilt and to call for compensation. (I am not the only parent who, having shouted unnecessarily at a son, has attempted to make it up to him with an apology and a trip to a doughnut shop—the latter receiving much the better hearing.) If compensation of some kind is *not* forthcoming, the metaphor of unpaid debt again seems warranted. In short, it seems impossible that we could live together with other people without constantly incurring debts—of one kind or another—to them, and they to us.

We can, of course, simply ignore such claims, but we are not, it seems, playing fair if we do so. Those we harm are *due* some reparation; benefactors are *due* at least some token of appreciation. We may see these norms as inherent in the human condition apart from any mention of the supernatural. If, however, we allow that we owe our life, our world, and "every good gift and every perfect gift" to the bounty of the Creator, then it fol-

lows that we all have incurred an enormous (and largely undis-
charged) debt to God as well.[1] We have scarcely given God due
recognition for his favors. If, moreover, other human beings are
God's creatures, then our debt to God increases with each wrong
we do to them. Furthermore, if we ourselves are the handiwork
of a wise and good Creator, then
presumably such a Creator must
have intended something more
(and rather different) to be made
of our own lives than sober intro-
spection will allow that we have
achieved; our guilt toward God
must include our distorted goals
and sullied ideals.

> It seems impossible that we could live together with other people without constantly incurring debts—of one kind or another—to them, and they to us.

Such a debt to God and others ought not simply to be ignored:
that would be to turn a blind eye to the most basic truths about
the human presence in God's world. On the other hand, it is,
presumably, God's prerogative to spell out what he requires if
we would be rid of our debt to him. But Jewish and Christian
tradition goes further. Convinced as it is of God's goodwill toward humankind, it declares that God himself has graciously
made available the means for humans to have their indebtedness
absolved, their guilt toward God removed; they need only avail
themselves of the divine provision. Conversely, to refuse such a
response is necessarily to retain one's indebtedness—indeed, to
compound it with contempt for the goodness of God.

An Added Dimension

Along some such lines we may approximate biblical notions
of guilt and atonement. To enter more fully into the latter field
of vision, we need not discount anything of what has been said.
We will, however, need to add a further dimension.

For us, the nonhuman world serves as the unnoticed stage on
which humans live out their significant lives. Unless nature ("*our*
environment," as we not so modestly label it) is the direct target
of our activities, we think it not a party to what we do—any more
than we think of ourselves as part of nature. Should some crime

1. James 1:17 KJV.

be committed, it may or may not be detected by the relevant (*human*) authorities. If they detect it, they may or may not choose to prosecute. If they prosecute, they may or may not choose to punish. In any case, a competent judge must determine the punishment to be assigned. Undetected, unprosecuted, or unpunished crimes are commonly thought to bear no consequences.

The biblical view is of course very different. One obvious reason for the difference is that, in the Bible, *God* is seen as the ultimate Judge of all our behavior: wrongdoing, then, can never go undetected, nor is it ever simply disregarded. But another and more

---

In the biblical view, just as wrongdoing corrupts nature, so the restoration of justice and peace among human beings will bring harmony to nature.

> The wolf shall live with the lamb,
>> the leopard shall lie down with the kid,
>
> the calf and the lion and the fatling together,
>> and a little child shall lead them.
>
> The cow and the bear shall graze,
>> their young shall lie down together;
>> and the lion shall eat straw like the ox.
>
> The nursing child shall play over the hole of the asp,
>> and the weaned child shall put its hand on the adder's den.
>
> They will not hurt or destroy on all my holy mountain;
>
> for the earth will be full of the knowledge of the LORD
>> as the waters cover the sea.
>
> Isaiah 11:6–9 NRSV

---

subtle reason for the difference lies in the biblical view of humanity's vital place *within* God's creation. Nonhuman nature is no mere backdrop for human behavior; it is itself charged with divine goodness: "The whole earth is full of [God's] glory."[2] The ordinary course of nature displays and celebrates God's faithfulness to his creation. In a world of goodness, however, human self-absorption

---

2. Isaiah 6:3 NRSV.

and heedless self-promotion represent an unwanted intrusion, a sordid violation of all that is innocent and good. Nature itself inevitably suffers when humans flout its order. Thus, the earth that witnessed Adam's rebellion bore him thorns and thistles.[3] After swallowing Abel's blood, it yielded no fruit for his murderer.[4] Famine decimated the land when the king failed to keep an oath.[5]

A telling reflection of the difference between the biblical perspective and our own is the use in Hebrew of a single word where we require two for "misdeed" and "punishment." Note, for example, that when Cain learns that the earth that has absorbed his brother's blood will never provide him a refuge, he declares (literally) that his "iniquity" (in Hebrew, *not* a distinct word for "punishment") is more than he can bear.[6] Should Israelites renege on a solemn commitment, they can be sure that their "sin" (*not* an arbitrarily affixed punishment) will "find [them] out" (it will come back to haunt them).[7] For those who see themselves living in a value-neutral, purely material universe, the only negative consequence of misdeeds that they can envisage is an assigned punishment; and since punishment does not follow every crime, a verbal distinction between "crime" and "punishment" is required. In the divinely charged nature of biblical horizons, however, wrongdoing is a disturbance of the good that cannot but have evil consequences. The sinful act and its inevitable sequel are two stages in a single process—for which a single word ("sin" or "iniquity") will do. What Cain laments is thus not the harshness of the punishment imposed upon him, but his own iniquity, the enormity of whose bane he had not anticipated. Even when the Hebrew law codes spell out what should be done to wrongdoers, the underlying notion is the same: wrongdoing brings disaster. The administration of justice merely assures that the wrongdoers themselves are the ones who experience its brunt. They are thus made to "bear" (not "their punishment," but) their "iniquity."[8] By another graphic turn of phrase, God is said to bring their "sin" down upon their own "head."[9]

3. Genesis 3:17–18.
4. Genesis 4:11–12.
5. Second Samuel 21:1.
6. Genesis 4:13.
7. Numbers 32:23.
8. Leviticus 17:16.
9. First Kings 2:32–33; 8:32.

If, then, a benevolent deity wishes to deliver humans from the bane of their guilt, he cannot simply overlook their misdeeds. The latter option would be excluded in any case by the divine *tzedakah,* God's unswerving faithfulness in upholding (or restoring) the goodness of his creation: divine goodness cannot be indifferent to evil. But, beyond that necessity of the Lord's "righteousness," divine disregard for sin would do nothing to interrupt the fatal link between its two stages. The incursion of sin must be countered, its contamination expunged. The divine solution is "atonement." In the Hebrew Scriptures, God designates a sacrificial animal as the substitute victim on whom the bane of human sin can be directed and exhausted. This remedy avoids any suggestion that God overlooks the distinction between good and evil, or that he condones sin. At the same time it provides for humans deliverance from the consequences of their iniquities. All that is required on their side is faithful participation in the ceremonies of atonement. They thus make their own the means that God has provided for their absolution.[10]

The preceding summary is, of course, too simple, straightforward, and even mechanical to do justice to reality as the ancient Israelites themselves conceived it. They were abundantly aware that human relationships are so interwoven that many people suffer the bane of sins for which they bear no personal responsibility.[11] And no doubt it was largely when nature posed an extraordinary threat to human well-being that people sought out specific acts of wrongdoing as the cause. Nonetheless, the following convictions seem both basic and common within biblical horizons.

1. Humans sin—even the best of them.
2. Sin brings bane upon human affairs.
3. Nature suffers as well.[12]
4. Sin must be atoned for if its bane is to be broken.
5. God, in his continued goodness toward his sinful creatures, provides for the atonement of their sins.

10. See Leviticus 4:1–6:7; 16:1–34.
11. See Exodus 20:5; 2 Samuel 24:17.
12. Note Paul's claim in Romans 8:13–23 that God has consigned creation to the suffering of decay and futility as long as humans bear the marks of sin.

Early Christian Perspectives

When the early Christians spoke of Jesus' death, they took over the language of atonement used in the Hebrew Scriptures.[13] Of course, if Jesus' death was needed to atone for human sins, then Israel's rites of atonement must not have been (or at least must no longer be) adequate for the job.[14] The early Christians did not need to deny that God had established the latter; a common alternative was to see them as preparatory, pedagogic devices: Israel's repeated sacrifices highlighted the crisis provoked by human sin, the divine willingness to forgive, and the necessity of an atoning sacrifice. In this way, though themselves far from a match for the sins of the world, Israel's rites foreshadowed the once-for-all, universally effective self-sacrifice of God's Son.[15] They were symbolic; he is the "[true] place [or means] of expiation" for the sin of all humankind.[16]

Paul's reference to atonement in our passage is rightly regarded as traditional, a reaffirmation of central Christian convictions. Five features of the Pauline restatement call for comment here.

> But now, apart from law, the righteousness of God has been disclosed, and is attested by the law and the prophets, the righteousness of God through faith in Jesus Christ for all who believe. For there is no distinction, since all have sinned and fall short of the glory of God; they are now justified by his grace as a gift, through the redemption that is in Christ Jesus, whom God put forward as a sacrifice of atonement by his blood, effective through faith. He did this to show his righteousness, because in his divine forbearance he had passed over the sins previously committed; it was to prove at the present time that he himself is righteous and that he justifies the one who has faith in Jesus.
>
> Romans 3:21–26 NRSV

13. Isaiah 53 provided an important intermediate step, much exploited by the early Christians. There the prophet speaks of a *human* "offering for sin" (verse 10), of a man upon whom "the LORD has laid . . . the iniquity of us all" (verse 6; note also the language of verses 5, 8, 11–12).

14. Note, e.g., Hebrews 10:4: "It is impossible for the blood of bulls and goats to take away sins."

15. See Hebrews 10:1–14; and note the language of 1 Corinthians 5:7 and Colossians 2:16–17. I will discuss the notion of divine sonship in chapter 7.

16. Romans 3:25; see John 1:29; 1 John 2:2.

1. Over the centuries atonement has often been portrayed as the ingenious means by which two opposing divine character-istics can both find satisfactory expression. Divine holiness (or justice) requires punishment for sin, whereas divine mercy re-quires that God save the sinner. The death of Christ, as a divinely provided substitute for the death deserved by sinners, is seen as allowing both of these divine attributes their proper function.

Such an interpretation, in spite of its venerable pedigree, cannot claim Paul as its progenitor. For Paul, the death of Christ represents, not the resolution of a tension within the Deity, but the solution to a *human* dilemma ("all have sinned") achieved by God's *tzedakah* ("righteousness"),[17] his faithful-ness in upholding creation's goodness. It is divine *tzedakah* that, in Christ's death, refuses to blur the distinction between good and evil by ignoring or trivializing the latter; how could God demonstrate more clearly the wrongfulness of human sin than by giving his Son's life as its atonement? "God put forward [Christ Jesus] as a sacrifice of atonement, . . . to show his righteousness, because in his divine forbearance he had [temporarily, before Christ came] passed over the sins previ-ously committed." But the same divine *tzedakah*, the same divine commitment to the goodness of his creation, is at work in the death of Christ to restore sinful humanity to its intended place in creation's order. "It was to prove at the present time that he himself is righteous and that he justifies the [sinner] who has faith in Jesus." In short, the message of Romans 3:21–26 is not that mercy triumphs over judgment, but that, in a world gone awry, divine goodness has reasserted itself, granting drastic recognition to the reality of sin, yet restor-ing God's sinful creatures to their intended place of glory in God's creation.

2. Those who know their sins to be atoned for are labeled (in Greek) *dikaioumenoi*: those who have been "declared righteous" (or "found innocent"; NRSV: "justified"). Since, in the ordinary use of the term, the "righteous" are contrasted with "sinners," there is a deliberate paradox in Paul's claim that God *declares* "sinners" to be "righteous": Paul is saying, in effect, that God

---

17. Paul uses the Greek word *dikaiosynē*, in his day a time-honored equivalent for the Hebrew term.

declares the guilty to be innocent![18] Such a declaration would represent a gross miscarriage of justice if it were not for the death of Christ. But God can *justly* declare sinners righteous since he has himself provided atonement for their sins: "God put forward [Christ Jesus] as a sacrifice of atonement, . . . to prove at the present time that he himself is righteous and that he justifies [or "declares righteous"] the one who has faith in Jesus." Christ bore the bane of their wrongdoing so that they need not do so. Now and at the final judgment God can find them innocent ("righteous").

3. Paul's concern here is not with human *feelings* of guilt, but with God's overcoming and expunging the (objective) guilt incurred by human sin. There are, no doubt, psychological benefits for those who know themselves to be guilty of sundry sins but who believe that God loves, forgives, and accepts them for the sake of Christ. Indeed, something of the kind may have been in Paul's mind when (on one reading of the text) he invites his readers in Romans 5:1 to "enjoy [their] peace with God." But the drama of sin and atonement in Romans 3 is not just a matter of bringing peace to guilt-ridden consciences. On the cross of Christ, God has dealt with the bane of sin that brings death to sinners and disfigures all creation.

4. The divine "redemption" (or "costly liberation") is made available in Christ Jesus to Jews and non-Jews alike. It is thus a reassertion of divine goodness toward, and sovereignty over, all humankind.[19] Jews were given the scrolls of the law; Gentiles were not. But humans of every race have sinned and relinquished their favored place in God's created order. The law drew attention to human rebellion against God's goodness but could not quell the rebellion. Now, "apart from [the] law,"[20] God's *tzedakah* has been demonstrated, and his offer to declare sinners "righteous" has been made available, to Jews and Gentiles alike. God (as Paul insists that his gospel shows) is God of the Jews—and God of the Gentiles also.[21]

18. Romans 3:23–24; see also 4:5; 5:8–9.
19. Romans 3:22–24, 29–30.
20. Romans 3:21.
21. Romans 3:29.

5. The required human response is that of "faith." This latter topic is crucial and will occupy us in the next chapter, as it does Paul in Romans 4. For the moment we need only note that the required response does nothing, in Paul's mind, to jeopardize the nature of divine redemption as a gift granted freely to sinners by the grace of God.[22]

22. Romans 3:24.

6

Faith's Awakening

Romans 4:1–25

No theme is more important in Paul's Letter to the Romans than that of "faith." In this chapter, we consider faith's character, its model, and its place in Paul's thought.

Love's Awakening—and Faith

In an earlier chapter, Barb and Bob were singled out, perhaps unduly, for an honored place in the narrative. It is time I told of Tammy and Tom.

The mutual discovery of Barb and Bob, you recall, was quite unexpected. Indeed, had they been on the "lookout," Barb would not have dreamed of looking in Bob's direction, nor Bob in Barb's. They had known each other, and taken each other for granted, too long for that. Each thought decently enough of the other. But they did so seldom—and *never* in romantic terms. Until, that is, they found themselves together one afternoon discussing some trivial incident that had taken place in their town, . . . and their eyes were opened, and the world changed forever its accustomed hue.

The story of Tammy and Tom is a little different. Tom, feel-ing isolated by the strange change that had come over Bob and a score of his other friends, had begun a search in earnest for *his* "Barb." Likewise, Tammy noticed a change in Barb. More significant in her case, however, was the knowledge she had acquired—from absorbing a thousand movies and skimming a good half-dozen books—of precisely how things were sup-posed to happen for a girl of her age and practiced charms. As a result, she was eagerly awaiting the appearance of someone (the hackneyed phrase "the right person" is here perhaps overly specific) with whom they could happen. And there was *Tom!* And *there* was Tammy!

What chiefly appealed to Tammy and Tom about Tom and Tammy, apart from their unmistakable availability, was the evi-dent interest each of them had in being half of a "Tammy and Tom." They played their parts with the consummate ease of those who had rehearsed every line and gesture in a thousand wakeful dreams. Full attention was required only to see that the proper proper names ("O Tom! Tom!" "Yes, Tammy!") were inserted at crucial junctures; and—rest assured, anxious Reader!—they were equal to the task, though their preoccupation with their own part would no doubt have blinded them in any case to the slips of their fellow actor. Charitably inclined as we are—and having once been young ourselves—we will leave them with the wish that when, in the course of the next several months, they actually begin the process of discovering each other, they will like what they see.

For Barb and Bob's experience we felt justified in dusting off a well-worn tag: they had "fallen in love" with each other. Of Tammy and Tom, the most we can say is that they were in love with the *idea* of falling in love. Apart from his availability, Tom's character played little role in shaping Tammy's experience of their relationship, at least in its initial stages; nor did Tammy's personality figure largely in Tom's perturbation. Had Tammy's Tom been Tim, or Tom's Tammy a Tina, they would scarcely have noticed the difference.

The contrast with Barb and Bob is again marked. No doubt they exaggerate each other's perfections. But Bob's whole world, when he is with her and when he is not, is unquestionably fo-cused on Barb: *her* smile, *her* voice, *her* eyes, *her* wit, *her* gait, *her* love. And Barb's thoughts are overwhelmed with Bob's *Bob*-ness. Suggest not to them that Barb could be Brenda, or Bob, Bill! There is, Bob would insist, nothing wrong with Brenda: but she is not *Barb*. Nor, in Barb's beholding, is Bill, Bob. Should it ever happen (the suggestion, for the moment, is heretical) that Barb and Bob have a falling out, and Barb should "fall in love" with Bill and Bob with Brenda, they will feel even then—and quite rightly—that neither "Barb and Bill" nor "Brenda and Bob" is the same as "Barb and Bob." The experience of falling in love *with someone* is inevitably as unique as are the personalities of those involved.

In short, love of a person is neither oblivious nor indifferent to the unique nature of the person loved. We may appropriately speak of our *love* for different people (a grandparent and an aunt, a parent and a child, a spouse and a friend), and even for pets. We are saying that we care deeply for them all, that we are committed to their well-being. Still, our love for each is elicited, experienced, and expressed in ways peculiar to each relationship. Love is impossible without an object, and the nature of love's object colors the nature of the love.

> Faith, like love, is elicited, experienced, and expressed in ways dependent upon its object. One may trust an exceptional politician, but not in quite the same way one trusts a parent, or a spouse, or a friend—or God.

The same is true of faith (or "trust"):[1] one trusts *someone* (or *something*) one has found, or has reason to believe, trust*worthy*. In requiring an object, then, *trust* is like love: it, too, is elicited, experienced, and expressed in ways dependent upon its object. One *may* trust an exceptional politician, but not in quite the same way one trusts a parent, or a spouse, or a friend—or God.

Now, one can *decide* to act as though one trusted someone, much as Tammy and Tom *decided* to play the role of those who have fallen in love—and it mattered little with whom they did so! But *true* trust, like (Barb and Bob's) love, does not come about

---

1. The Greek word *pistis* is used both for "faith, trust, confidence" and for "faithfulness, loyalty, reliability." In the corpus of his extant writings, Paul has occasion to use the word in both senses. Our immediate concern, however, is with the former usage.

through a simple decision made by the one who trusts. *True*
trust is a response elicited by the trust*worthiness* or goodness
of the one trusted; and the strength and character of *true* trust
inevitably depend on our perception of the character of the one
we trust. Ask those who have fallen in love why they have done
so, and they are likely to respond, not in terms of their own deci-
sion-making process (they will hardly allow that they decided to
fall in love!), but simply with what they find lovable about the
object of their devotion. Ask those who trust why they do so,
and their answer will indicate what they find worthy of trust in
the object of their faith.

Faith and Father Abraham

Paul cites Abraham (in the Genesis account, he is called first
"Abram," then "Abraham") as the "father" of all who believe.[2]
To understand Paul, we must consider Abraham.

Abraham's story begins in earnest in Genesis 12 with a strik-
ing divine commission:

> The LORD said to Abram, "Set forth from your land, your kinsfolk,
> and your father's household, for a land that I will show you. And
> I will make of you a great nation. I will bless you and make your
> name great, and you will become a standard of blessing. I will bless
> those who bless you and curse those who curse you. All the earth's
> clans, when they bless themselves, will use you as the standard of
> blessing" [or, "All the earth's clans will be blessed in you"].[3]

The laconic narrative continues, "And Abram set forth as the
LORD had told him";[4] and we may well see his behavior at the
outset as a model of obedience to God. Still, his obedience was
clearly preceded and motivated by an equally exemplary *trust:*
Abram sets out for an undisclosed destination on God's verbal
assurance that (1) he will show it to Abram in good time, (2) there
Abram will become the founder of a great nation and (3) be
abundantly "blessed" (4) to the point that his name will be used
proverbially as one who is a favorite with God. The promises

2. Romans 4:11–12; also Galatians 3:7.
3. Genesis 12:1–3.
4. Genesis 12:4.

are incredible; yet, if Abram is to act upon them, he must deem
them—and the divine promise-Giver—trustworthy. Abram necessarily *trusted* God when he obeyed God as he did.

In the stories that follow, Abram's obedience is somewhat
spotty: it lags where his faith flags. Twice he lies about Sarah
his wife, calling her his sister out of fear for his life—though
God's yet unfulfilled promises require his survival.[5] In Genesis
16, Abram (at his wife's prompting) decides that God's initiative
requires some (rather devious) assistance if it is ever to come
to anything. On the other hand, when his prayer of despair is
met, not with divine action, but with a still more incredible restatement of the divine promise, Abram, we are told, "believed
the LORD; and the LORD credited it to him as righteousness."[6]
And Abraham's faith passes a still more stupefying test when
he trusts God even though the latter commands the sacrifice
of his son.[7]

Scripture portrays Abraham as God's intimate "friend," one
who "walked" with God, "stood" before God, was kept apprised
of God's plans, and was even allowed a part in their formation.[8]
Such a relationship bred and reflected the trust for which Abraham serves as a Pauline model.

The Place of Faith in Paul

In the "Jewish-Christian" vision,[9] God is worthy of our trust.
When humans set out on an independent path dictated by their
own interests and ambitions, they signal their *dis*trust in God.
But if we grant the truth of Paul's gospel of divine redemption, then what God has done in Christ has been (among other
things) to furnish a fresh and prodigious demonstration that
he is worthy of human trust. So great has been God's commitment to restoring the goodness of creation, and so strong has
been his love for humankind, that he himself has provided a
costly atonement for the sins of those who have wronged him.

---

5. Genesis 12:10–20; 20:1–18.

6. Genesis 15:2–6.

7. Genesis 22:1–14. The narrative goes on to say that in the end the sacrifice
was not required.

8. Isaiah 41:8; Genesis 17:1; 18:17–33.

9. For the sense in which I use the phrase, see chapter 1, note 7.

The natural, appropriate response evoked by the proclamation of the Christian message should thus be faith, or trust, in God: faith is awakened by hearing the word of Christ.[10]

A few observations are in order.

1. Paul can speak both of "believing *in*" God[11] and of "believing *that* God raised [Christ] from the dead."[12] These two types of faith—(a) confidence in a person and (b) the conviction that a particular claim is true—are not as distinct as they are sometimes made out to be. Humans (according to the "Jewish-Christian" vision) should trust God but do not. They learn once again what it is to trust God (type a, above) when they take seriously (or *believe*) the content of some claim that proves him to be trustworthy (type b, above). A fine example is offered by Exodus 14:31: Israel's faith in God (and in Moses his servant) was kindled by the people seeing (and believing!) that the Lord had delivered them from the Egyptians. Similarly, for Paul, the belief that God has acted on our behalf in Christ awakens a proper trust in God: "We are those who trust in [God], who raised Jesus our Lord from the dead, who was handed over for our transgressions and raised so that we might be declared righteous."[13] Appropriate faith in God thus follows from the conviction that the Christian message of what he has done is true.[14]

2. God's demonstration of his trustworthiness in Christ is thus the means, not merely of atoning for human sins, but also of spurring rebellious humans to a living faith in God. On the other hand, the proclamation of Christ's death as the atonement for human sin cannot benefit those who do not respond in faith.

The natural, appropriate response evoked by the proclamation of the Christian message should thus be faith, or trust, in God: faith is awakened by hearing the word of Christ.

10. Romans 10:17.

11. Romans 4:3, 5; 10:11. The Greek verb is *pisteuō*, related to the noun *pistis*, "faith" or "trust."

12. Romans 10:9.

13. Romans 4:24–25.

14. First Peter 1:21 provides a good summary of the point: "*By Christ* you believe *in God*, who raised him from the dead and gave him glory, *so that your faith and hope might be in God*."

By continuing to act like gods in their own world rather than trust God in his, they persist in the very lie that breeds the sins for which Christ died.

3. For Paul, the "righteousness" that God grants sinners who believe the gospel is a gift; it is not something that they themselves have earned. It would be different if God had approved them (or declared them "righteous") because they themselves had always done the right thing: God would simply be recognizing a righteousness for which they could take the credit. But since

> What then are we to say was gained by Abraham, our ancestor according to the flesh? For if Abraham was justified [or declared righteous] by works, he has something to boast about, but not before God. For what does the scripture say? "Abraham believed God, and it was reckoned to him as righteousness." Now to one who works, wages are not reckoned as a gift but as something due. But to one who without works trusts him who justifies [declares righteous] the ungodly, such faith is reckoned as righteousness. So also David speaks of the blessedness of those to whom God reckons righteousness apart from works:
>
> > "Blessed are those whose iniquities are forgiven,
> >   and whose sins are covered;
> > blessed is the one against whom
> >   the Lord will not reckon sin."
>
> Romans 4:1–8 NRSV

the people God declares righteous are themselves "sinners," the "ungodly," those who had lived as God's "enemies";[15] and since it is only because Christ atoned for their sins that God can declare them righteous, they can claim no credit for the declaration. People who receive a gift are not to be confused with those who receive compensation for what they have done. The righteousness offered in the gospel is not a reward for the righteous "works" that people have done, but a gift of God's grace to sinners.[16]

15. Romans 4:5; 5:6, 8, 10.
16. Romans 4:1–8.

4. On the other hand, we must not take Paul's well-known contrast between faith and works, and his insistence that only the former is involved when God declares *sinners* righteous, as permitting those who have been declared righteous to live as they please. Paul is adamant that faith in God must find expression[17] in appropriate deeds: after all, those who do not *obey* God cannot be said to trust him, since they rely more on their own judgment of what is best than on God's.[18] In Paul's mind, however, deeds that express a believer's faith are distinct from the works that, he insists, play no role when God declares *sinners* righteous. Sinners, after all, have no righteous works that God can recognize. But those who respond to God's salvation in faith, and whom God has *declared* righteous, are now bound to express their newfound trust in God by obeying him. Their very acts of obedience, Paul adds, are inspired and empowered by God's grace.[19]

5. Paul can speak as though "faith" began with the coming of Christ,[20] a claim that seems consistent with the view that humanity, apart from Christ, is in a state of rebellion against God. On the other hand, he does allow Abraham as a model of Christian faith: a common pattern is seen in that Abraham, like the Christian, was *declared* righteous, not because he had done what is right, but because he responded with faith to an initiative of God's grace.[21]

17. Note, for example, the phrase "obedience of faith" in Romans 1:5: those who trust God can be counted on to obey him. What really matters, according to Galatians 5:6, is "faith *that is active in love.*"

18. See Romans 8:13; 2 Corinthians 5:10. See also chapters 8 and 12, below.

19. First Corinthians 15:9–10; 2 Corinthians 12:9–10; Romans 8:13–14; Galatians 5:16–25.

20. Galatians 3:23, 25.

21. Romans 4:3–5, 17–22. Galatians 3:8 can be construed as saying that Abraham himself was a believer in the Christian gospel inasmuch as it was implicit in the divine promises given him. Such a reading would corroborate the claim that faith is necessarily linked to the coming of Christ, even among those who lived before his appearing. In any case Paul does not believe that all who lived prior to Christ were simply condemned. Without elaborating the point, he speaks of the time prior to Christ's death as one of divine "forbearance." That sins were then temporarily "passed over," not condoned, is demonstrated by the event that brought the period of "forbearance" to an end: the atoning death of Christ (Romans 3:25–26).

6. Paul stresses once again in Romans 4 that the same path of faith is open to Jews and non-Jews alike. Abraham serves as the model and "father" of all who believe, whether they are circumcised Jews or uncircumcised Gentiles: he himself believed and was declared righteous while he was still uncircumcised.[22] Later God gave the law to Israel; but God never meant (Paul insists) to limit the blessing of Abraham to those who received the law. Those who think he did in fact set aside faith as the criterion of blessing,[23] misconstrue the actual effect of the law (which was to pronounce judgment on its transgressors),[24] and limit the blessings that God promised to *all* of Abraham's descendants to a single nation—contrary to the very terms of the initial commitment: "I have made you a father of many nations."[25] The story of Abraham, Paul concludes, has been recorded for the benefit of *all* who believe in, and are declared righteous by, the God who raised Jesus from the dead.[26]

22. Romans 4:9–12.
23. Romans 4:13–14.
24. Romans 4:15.
25. Romans 4:16–17.
26. Romans 4:23–25.

7

Just Cause for Joy

Romans 5:1–11

W hat God has done for us through Christ should move us to trust him: faith is, for Paul, the appropriate human response to the gospel. But, Paul assures us, the gospel also evokes joy.

Of Goodness and Joy

No doubt the closest analogy to what Paul means is, again, provided by the experience of human love that is enthralled with its beloved, and at the same time has come to view the world itself as home to a goodness and beauty it had not dreamed existed. With the discovery comes joy: a profound sense of the goodness of life in which one is accepted, welcomed, even loved by the other who matters most in all the world.

The psalmists of the Bible found joy in the presence of God: an overwhelming sense that, wherever one found oneself,[1] and what-

1. See Psalm 139.

ever one's circumstances, God is there—and God is good.[2] The joy
may be expressed, as the Psalms frequently enjoin, with music and
dance and boisterous shouts. It may find voice in a quiet prayer of
assurance: "When I awake, I am still with thee."[3] In any case, the
psalmists repeatedly speak of discovering in the Eternal not only
their provision and protection but also their heart's delight:

> Thou hast put gladness in my heart,
>> more than in the time
>>> that their corn and their wine increased.[4]

> In thy presence is fullness of joy;
>> at thy right hand
>> there are pleasures for evermore.[5]

> Delight thyself also in the LORD;
>> and he shall give thee
>> the desires of thine heart.[6]

Not incidental to the pleasure was the belief that the enjoyment was mutual:

> He [God] delighteth not in the strength of the horse:
>> he taketh not pleasure in the legs of a man.
> The LORD taketh pleasure in them that fear him,
>> in those that hope in his mercy.[7]

The psalmists' joy is rooted in their conviction that, circumstances notwithstanding, life is good, and that they have a share
in its goodness, loved by the One who matters most. Praise, for
them, is the natural, appropriate venting of joy: to praise the
Lord is "fitting" and "good."[8]

For his part, Paul believes (as we have seen) that a spirit
of rebellion has infected all humankind, and done so with di-

2. See the discussion of the Psalms in chapter 2, above.
3. Psalm 139:18 KJV.
4. Psalm 4:7 KJV.
5. Psalm 16:11 KJV.
6. Psalm 37:4 KJV.
7. Psalm 147:10–11 KJV.
8. Psalm 92:1; 147:1.

sastrous effect; but also that God has reasserted his *tzedakah*,[9] provided atonement for the ravages of sin, and in the process summoned humanity to return to the embrace of his goodness. To trust the God who has demonstrated his love in Christ is to be "reconciled" to him, to be "at peace" with him and restored

> Therefore, since we are justified by faith, we have peace with God through our Lord Jesus Christ, through whom we have obtained access to this grace in which we stand; and we boast in our hope of sharing the glory of God. And not only that, but we also boast in our sufferings, knowing that suffering produces endurance, and endurance produces character, and character produces hope, and hope does not disappoint us, because God's love has been poured into our hearts through the Holy Spirit that has been given to us.
>
> For while we were still weak, at the right time Christ died for the ungodly. Indeed, rarely will anyone die for a righteous person—though perhaps for a good person someone might actually dare to die. But God proves his love for us in that while we still were sinners Christ died for us. Much more surely then, now that we have been justified by his blood, will we be saved through him from the wrath of God. For if while we were enemies, we were reconciled to God through the death of his Son, much more surely, having been reconciled, will we be saved by his life. But more than that, we even boast in God through our Lord Jesus Christ, through whom we have now received reconciliation.
>
> Romans 5:1–11 NRSV

to his good graces, and, at the same time, to be assured of a share in God's eternal glory:[10] cause enough, Paul declares, for exuberant celebration.[11]

9. For the term, see chapter 2, above.
10. Romans 5:1–2, 10.
11. Romans 5:11.

This celebration can continue whatever one's outward circumstances:[12] the latter cannot imperil one's place in the divine favor. Paul provides several grounds for persistent joy.

First, even hard times serve a purpose, strengthening and proving the mettle of those who endure them and sharpening their hope for deliverance from distresses that are an inevitable part of life in a creation marred by sin: "We also boast in our sufferings, knowing that suffering produces endurance."[13]

Second, when Christians hope for the deliverance and glory that God has promised, their hope is one that will not disappoint them. God is not one to let people down, and believers already know in their hearts that God loves them: "Hope does not disappoint us, because God's love has been poured into our hearts through the Holy Spirit that has been given to us."[14]

The Roman Christians, Paul assumes, know the Spirit and the experience he speaks of. No academic discussion can convey the experience. But something should be said about Paul's understanding of the Spirit.

Joy and the Spirit

The Hebrew Scriptures contain a number of accounts in which the spirit of God is said to come upon individuals, inducing at times eccentric behavior,[15] but also enabling those who receive the spirit to accomplish feats beyond their normal capacities. A gift for prophecy[16] and the performance of extraordinary exploits in battle[17] are at times attributed to the onrush of God's spirit, though the presence of the spirit could be seen in more temperate endowments as well.[18] Not surprisingly, an ideal took shape that envisioned the day when all God's people would possess his spirit.[19] *All* would then prophesy. And perhaps, as Ezekiel ventured to forecast, God's people, in possession of God's spirit,

12. Romans 5:3.
13. Romans 5:2–4; see also Romans 8:18–39.
14. Romans 5:5.
15. See, for example, 1 Samuel 19:20–24.
16. Numbers 11:25–26.
17. Judges 3:10.
18. Exodus 35:30–35.
19. Numbers 11:29; Joel 2:28–29.

might even prove able, in spite of their wayward past, to obey God's laws.[20]

The beginnings of the Christian movement were accompanied by charismatic outbreaks interpreted as evidence that this prophetic vision had been fulfilled: God's spirit had been poured out upon God's people.[21] This conviction was central to Paul's Christian thought. Every believer in Christ, he insisted, was in possession of the Spirit.[22] Indeed, the gift of the Spirit represented for Paul a first installment, or guarantee, of the full glory still in store for believers.[23] It empowered Christian ethical behavior[24] and equipped individual believers to make their own distinctive contribution to the well-being of the community as a whole.[25]

> I will pour out my spirit on all flesh;
> your sons and your daughters shall prophesy.
>
> Joel 2:28 NRSV
>
> I will put my spirit within you,
> and make you follow my statutes
> and be careful to observe my ordinances.
>
> Ezekiel 36:27 NRSV

But the divine Spirit given to believers was also seen (and this is the point in the passage we are considering) as the source of their experience of the divine Presence, both in their community gatherings[26] and in their private devotion. In their weakness (Paul writes in Romans 8), believers sense the help of the Spirit, bearing their prayers into the presence of God with sighs too deep for words.[27] The same Spirit's quiet testimony in their hearts gives believers treasured assurance of their acceptance as God's children.[28] In our passage, it is the reality of God's love for his children that the Spirit conveys to their hearts; assured

20. Ezekiel 36:27.
21. Acts 2:1–18; 1 Corinthians 12:7–11.
22. Romans 8:9.
23. Romans 8:23; 2 Corinthians 1:22; 5:5.
24. Romans 7:6; 8:4; Galatians 5:16–25. Note the parallel to Ezekiel's forecast mentioned above.
25. First Corinthians 12:4–11.
26. Note the reference to the "communion [or fellowship] of the Holy Spirit" in 2 Corinthians 13:13.
27. Romans 8:26.
28. Romans 8:14–16; also Galatians 4:6.

that God loves them now, they need not doubt God's promises
of bliss to come.

Paul can speak in one breath of the Spirit "of God," in another
of the Spirit "of Christ."[29] Only one Spirit is meant: it conveys
to the hearts of believers a sense of
the love of *God* that was displayed
in the life and death of *Christ*. At
the same time, Paul regularly distinguishes between God and the
Spirit[30] and between Christ and the
Spirit.[31] Indeed, there are formulas
in Paul in which the three (God/
the Father, Christ/the Son, and
the Spirit/Holy Spirit) are listed
side by side, most famously that
invoking the blessing of the "Lord
Jesus Christ," "God," and the "Holy
Spirit" on the Corinthian believers
in 2 Corinthians 13:13.[32]

> The Spirit of God dwells in you.
> Anyone who does not have the
> Spirit of Christ does not belong to
> him.
>
> Romans 8:9 NRSV
>
> [God] has anointed us, by putting
> his seal on us and giving us his
> Spirit in our hearts as a first
> installment.
>
> 2 Corinthians 1:21–22 NRSV
>
> God [sent] . . . his own Son . . . to
> deal with sin, . . . so that the just
> requirement of the law might
> be fulfilled in us, who walk
> not according to the flesh but
> according to the Spirit.
>
> Romans 8:3–4 NRSV
>
> Now there are varieties of gifts,
> but the same Spirit. . . . To each
> is given the manifestation of the
> Spirit for the common good.
>
> 1 Corinthians 12:4, 7 NRSV

The church of a later day, when
defining, communicating, and de-
fending its faith, felt constrained
to insist that the "one God" (or the
God who was "one" in "substance"
or "essence") was existent in the
"three persons" of the "Trinity."
Thus they expressed the distinction within the Deity required by
the revelation of a God who had
acted in Christ and was now present in the Holy Spirit. Paul himself had no such ready formulas
at hand, nor did he need them. Still, it must be said that the
later church was striving to find formulations that did justice

29. See, for example, Romans 8:9, 14.

30. For example, the Spirit (as noted above) is said to convey *to* God the
prayers of believers (Romans 8:26).

31. See, for example, the distinction in Romans 8:11.

32. See also Romans 8:3–4; and (with remarkable compactness) Galatians
4:6.

to features present in the Pauline texts—or, better, to the Reality that they believed underlay them.

The sense of God's love conveyed by God's Spirit is, then, Paul's second reason why believers can experience joy, whatever their circumstances. A third reason is found in yet another proof of the extent of God's love: God's *Son* gave his life for people when they were at their very worst: when they were still "weak," "ungodly," "sinners," God's "enemies." Since his love did not abandon them then, it is unthinkable that it would do so now, when they have been "reconciled" to God and enjoy his favor.[33]

God's Son died for sinners. We have seen what Paul means by sinners. But what is the point of calling Jesus God's *"Son"*?

The Proof of Divine Love—and the Divine Son

According to biblical tradition, the first monarch to rule over the united Israelite tribes was Saul: tall of stature, short in counsel, moody, suspicious, increasingly isolated, ultimately abandoned by God to his foes.[34] Succeeding him was not his son, but David, a court musician and, of course, the original giant-killer. The prophet Nathan declared to David that God would establish his dynasty forever and be a father to David's son, never abandoning him as he had abandoned Saul.[35] The oracle was the subject of several psalms which celebrated the divine "sonship" of Israel's Davidic king.[36] The

> I [God] will raise up your [David's] offspring after you, . . . and I will establish the throne of his kingdom forever. I will be a father to him, and he shall be a son to me. . . . Your house and your kingdom shall be made sure forever before me; your throne shall be established forever.
>
> 2 Samuel 7:12–16 NRSV

metaphor "God's son" spoke of the divine favor enjoyed by the king—*and* (no doubt) of the king's responsibility to carry out God's mandate of establishing justice.[37]

33. Romans 5:6–11.
34. First Samuel 8–31.
35. Second Samuel 7:12–16.
36. See Psalm 2, especially verse 7; Psalm 89:1–37, especially verses 26–27; also Psalm 132.
37. See Psalm 72.

God's sons in intention, the Davidic monarchs (on the whole) proved disappointingly human in the corruption with which they ruled. They were denounced by the prophets with the bitterness that betokens dashed ideals.[38] Prophets themselves foretold the fall of the Israelite kingdoms.[39] Still—we have seen this before—the dynamic of Israelite faith in a deity both powerful and benevolent did not allow that divine purposes could, in the end, be frustrated by human sin. Though the Davidic kings had proved unworthy of their calling, God would nonetheless fulfill his commitment to David and make of it—as intended—an instrument of his goodness. He would raise up in the future a righteous descendant of David to rule his people (or even the whole earth); evil would then be judged, Israel's oppressors would be overthrown, fear would be banished, and peace would accompany justice.[40] The hope for such a "messiah" (or "anointed" king) was entertained by a number of pious Jews in the time of Jesus.[41] Since Davidic kings of old had been declared "God's son," it would be natural if the same title should be used of the coming Davidic messiah; and there is some evidence that this was done.[42]

> The days are surely coming, says the LORD, when I will raise up for David a righteous Branch, and he shall reign as king and deal wisely, and shall execute justice and righteousness in the land. In his days Judah will be saved and Israel will live in safety. And this is the name by which he will be called: "The LORD is our righteousness."
>
> Jeremiah 23:5–6 NRSV

Central to early *Christ*ian faith was the conviction that Jesus was God's *Christ* (the Greek equivalent of the Hebrew "messiah"), the one through whom God was working to end the sway of evil

---

38. See, for example, Jeremiah 22; Ezekiel 34.

39. The southern kingdom, Judah, retained a Davidic monarch until its overthrow by the Babylonians.

40. See Isaiah 9:6–7; 11:1–10; Jeremiah 23:5–6; Ezekiel 34:23–31; Micah 5:2–4.

41. Note, however, that Israel's "messianic" hope included a *variety* of scenarios in which God would establish the rule of righteousness and restore the fortunes of his people. Not all of them featured a Davidic monarchy.

42. In the New Testament, note the apparent equivalence of the two titles in Mark 14:61; John 20:31.

and establish the rule of righteousness and peace. That messiah's atoning death was required for the change to take place was at least not a common belief among Jews in Jesus' day. Sin and evil must certainly be dealt with; but a more standard script required only that God would judge the wicked and deliver the righteous from their clutches. The early Christian drama implied, on the contrary, that *none* was fit to participate in God's rule apart from the atonement of their sin and a change of their heart's orientation: clearly a more radical view of human sin. At the same time, the divine intervention to establish peace and justice is also, in its Christian version, perhaps first and foremost a demonstration of divine *love,* partly in the length to which God was prepared to go to redeem humanity (involving, as it did, the death of God's "Christ"), partly in its inclusiveness (*all* are seen as "ungodly," and atonement is made for the sins of *all*).

To conclude this summary of the Christian *messianic* drama, we need only note that in proclaiming Jesus as "Christ," the early Christians were by no means limiting his role to his sacrificial death for others. The *risen* Christ was declared to be "Lord,"[43] the one through whom God administers his righteous rule. Even now their exalted Lord was at God's "right hand."[44] The open manifestation of his reign, and the decisive judgment of all who continue to defy it, were believed to be reserved for a day when sinners had been given due opportunity to repent, and the period of God's patience was finally over; then would come the rule of righteousness and peace for which all creation yearns.[45]

The designation "God's Son" could thus be used as an equivalent of "God's Messiah," the man appointed by God to bring about the triumph of the good. But Paul clearly means more by the title. Note, for example, how "Jesus Christ" is emphatically distinguished *from* human beings and classed (in some unspecified way) with God himself when Paul claims to be "an apostle with a commission neither originating with human beings, nor passed on by a human being, but given by Jesus Christ and God the Father."[46] Paul maintains the distinction throughout the

43. Acts 2:36; Romans 10:9; 1 Corinthians 12:3.
44. That is, he was God's administrator of universal affairs. See Acts 2:32–33; Ephesians 1:20–23.
45. Acts 3:19–21; 2 Peter 3:7–9; Romans 8:19–23.
46. Galatians 1:1.

verses that follow. He invokes divine blessing for human beings from "God our Father and the Lord Jesus Christ."[47] In carrying out his commission, Paul goes on to say, he could not please *people* and still serve *Christ*.[48] His gospel itself is not of human origin, nor was it communicated to him by any human being; it became his through a "revelation of Jesus Christ," a revelation of God's "Son."[49] The whole argument will not allow that "God's Son" is merely an honorary title for a human being with a divine task to fulfill.[50]

> It is crucial to Paul's argument that we see in the death of Jesus, not what a human being can do for God, but an expression of God's love for sinful humans.

Nor is it sufficient to say that for Paul the *man* Jesus had been exalted to something like divine status. While Paul certainly reckoned with the humanity of Jesus, he spoke of it as an adopted humanity, assumed for a divine purpose by one who himself existed previously "in the form of God."[51] Christ was "rich" before he became "poor" like us.[52] Romans is more explicit: "God accomplished what the law could not . . . by sending his Son in flesh like our sinful flesh."[53] It is, indeed, crucial to Paul's argument and gospel that we see in the death of Jesus, not what a human being can do for God, but an expression of God's love for sinful humans.[54] The exaltation of the risen Jesus thus represents for

47. Galatians 1:3. The double invocation is frequent in Paul.

48. Galatians 1:10.

49. Galatians 1:12, 16.

50. The passage (especially Galatians 1:15–16) also suggests that it was the appearance to Paul of the resurrected Jesus in divine glory that compelled him to speak of Christ in more exalted terms; compare 2 Corinthians 4:6, a verse that alludes to the same experience.

51. Philippians 2:5–7.

52. Second Corinthians 8:9.

53. Romans 8:3. The quoted material literally ends "in the likeness of flesh of sin." The awkward phrase is meant to convey the point that Christ, though human, was, unlike other humans, without sin. Compare 2 Corinthians 5:21 and (from a different early Christian author) Hebrews 4:15.

54. Romans 5:8. As we see in the next chapter, Paul does think that Christ's obedience *as a human being* overcame the effects of the sin of the first human being, Adam. But the very possibility of such "human" obedience depended on Christ's being something more than an offspring of Adam (see Romans 8:3).

Paul (as, of course, for the Fourth Gospel) the return of God's
Son to the glory he knew before he became a man.

Paul's language of Christ's divine "sonship" therefore serves
a number of purposes. It allows him to distinguish between
Christ and the "Father," who sent him to reconcile sinners to
himself. It suggests, moreover, the willing submission of the
"Son" to the "Father's" will.[55] At the same time, the term implies
that the divine "Son" is distinct from ordinary human beings
in sharing deity with the Father (as children share the nature
of their parents).[56]

Obviously, Paul is treading a fine line. Were we to say that only
Paul's Jewish heritage kept him from speaking of two (or three!)
gods, we would not do justice to the dynamic of his thinking.
God, for the Christian Paul, continued to be *one*, the benevolent
Creator of all. The life, death, and resurrection of Jesus Christ
were significant precisely because they represented an intervention by God the Creator to redeem his sinful creatures: a second
deity has no place in the scheme. Nor can Jesus be a mere man,
however, if his self-sacrifice is to represent the decisive revelation of God the Creator's love and goodness toward humanity.
Somehow terminology had to be found to express the conviction that creation and redemption are both the work of one God
while allowing (what the Christian experience of God required)
sufficient room for "otherness" within the Deity to accommodate
distinct roles within the same divine operations. Paul himself
offers nothing more precise than the following formulations:

> For us there is one God, the Father, *from* whom are all things and
> *for* whom we ourselves exist, and one Lord, Jesus Christ, *through*
> whom are all things—indeed, we ourselves live *through* him.[57]

> God was active in Christ, reconciling the world to himself.[58]

Hence the (human) obedience of Christ and its subsequent benefits are themselves
spoken of as a gift of God's grace to humanity (Romans 5:15).

55. See 1 Corinthians 15:28; Galatians 1:4.

56. A more explicit ascription of deity to Christ may be found in Romans 9:5,
a verse that—on its most natural reading—simply equates Christ with God. But
other interpretations of the verse are possible. Compare Colossians 2:9.

57. First Corinthians 8:6.

58. Second Corinthians 5:19.

God proves his love for us in that while we were still sinners Christ died for us.[59]

The later church would refine this language and see in the eternal relationship between Father, Son, and Holy Spirit a proof that God is eternally a God of love: even before there were *creatures* for God to love, the Father loved the Son; the Son loved the Father; both loved, and were loved by, the Holy Spirit. Such language carries us far beyond what we find in Paul—though, again, we may grant that it has roots in problems and features already found in the Pauline texts.

In any case Romans 5:10 is not concerned with details of Christian doctrine. The point is rather that Christians can be sure of the bliss God has promised when they remember the length to which God was prepared to go to make it possible: they were "reconciled to God through the death of his Son."[60]

59. Romans 5:8.
60. See the similar point in Romans 8:32.

8

Freedom versus Freedom

Romans 5:12–6:23

Neither birds in cages nor those with broken wings are *free* to fly. Nor will removing the cage of a bird with broken wings bring it its desired freedom; the wounded bird will be left an easy prey for its foes.

Contemporary notions of individual freedom stress release from external constraints: all "cages" must be removed so that people may act as they choose. Such notions of freedom are consistent with a worldview that sees human beings as the only source of meaning, significant order, and value in the world: they should be "free" to define for themselves what they find meaningful, to pursue what they themselves choose to value. Apart from the social contracts that make it possible for different people to live together, any externally imposed constraint on their freedom seems unwarranted and, for many, unwanted: Why should the preferences of others set limits for my behavior? What lies in the way of "free" individuals (provided it is not *another* "free" individual) may legitimately be bulldozed for their convenience.

Perceptive readers of the preceding chapters will harbor doubts as to whether Paul's notions of freedom can mesh with those of contemporary Western society. Sympathetic readers will hasten to add that his failure to see things as we do is not, in itself, sufficient cause for dismissing his views as absurd. The task of this chapter will be to define "freedom" as Paul uses the term and to explore the logic that links it to his "Jewish-Christian" horizons.

Freedom and Constraint in Paul

From Paul's perspective, the notion that people should be free to do as they please is wildly out of touch with reality. Human beings are but a part of a larger whole whose meaning, purposeful order, and goodness are *not* their creation. To bulldoze whatever obstructs their convenience is a most ill-considered way to make their presence felt in the cosmos as *God* created it: partly because their own well-being depends on the integrity of the whole; partly because the goodness inherent in the whole and in each of its parts merits human esteem, and people show themselves stupid, insensitive, or mean when they disregard or destroy it. Conversely, humans thrive as they embrace, celebrate, and pattern their lives according to the goodness of creation and the benevolent will of their Maker.

The moral laws that spell out *how* human beings may appropriately live in God's creation, and the institutions (marriage, the family, government) that foster and enforce such laws, provide the conditions within which humans flourish. To disregard them is to lose, not gain, one's freedom. Like birds with broken wings, human beings who refuse to accept their place in God's world are no longer *free* to enjoy life as it was meant to be lived. From their disastrous enslavement to the lie of their own independence, the self-absorbed need to be *set* free.

It is a lie that, according to the well-known story of Genesis 3, originated with Adam and Eve. They lived in, and were themselves a part of, the created order that God had declared "very good."[1] Within that order they enjoyed a privileged position, made in the "image of God" and exercising on his behalf

---

1. Genesis 1:31.

authority over other creatures.[2] They were placed in a garden pleasant to behold and bountiful in its provisions.[3] Their options were multitudinous—and all but one of them were good. Only a single command was given them so that they could acknowledge by their obedience their status as creatures in God's world: they were not to eat of the "tree of the knowledge of good and evil."[4] They ate, of course, distrusting the goodness of God and desiring to be "gods" themselves.[5] And so "sin entered into the world."[6]

> And the LORD God commanded the man, "You may freely eat of every tree of the garden; but of the tree of the knowledge of good and evil you shall not eat, for in the day that you eat of it you shall die."
> Genesis 2:16–17 NRSV

That the story of Adam[7] is in some sense the story of us all is certainly part of Paul's point in Romans 5:12–21; but the relationship between the wrongdoing of our progenitor and that of his discredited brood is not altogether clear. Romans 5:12 by itself might suggest simply that Adam was the first sinner, that his act introduced sin and death into our world, and that the rest of us share his fate inasmuch as we sin as he did. Adam, on such a reading, did us the disservice of setting a bad example—but we are fools to follow. We are under no particular pressure to do so. Each of us, in our own several ways, reenacts the disobedience and fall of our forebear in the garden of Eden.

> Sin came into the world through one man, and death came through sin, and so death spread to all because all have sinned.
> Romans 5:12 NRSV

2. Genesis 1:26–28.
3. Genesis 2:8–9, 15.
4. Genesis 2:17.
5. Genesis 3:4–6.
6. Romans 5:12.
7. Paul ignores the role of Eve in his references to the Genesis story in Romans 5:12–21, no doubt because he wants to focus on the comparison between Adam and Christ. Compare 1 Corinthians 15:21–22, 45; and contrast the reference to Eve in 2 Corinthians 11:3, where the comparison between Adam and Christ is not in view.

But such cannot be Paul's meaning. If we *all* do things that we ought not to do,[8] then there is more to be said about the human condition than that individuals make bad choices. The same conclusion follows if God is nowhere given the acknowledgment he is due.[9] In Romans 5:19 Paul speaks of the disobedience of Adam as the means by which others "were made sinners."[10] The implication is that, when people commit sins, they are not falling from innocence in the same way that Adam did; rather they are giving expression to the sinfulness that is characteristic of human nature in the post-Adam era. Paul can even say that people "live in sin":[11] sin is the sphere within which they act and think; it fixes the boundaries of their horizons. They choose to do, and are responsible for, the particular sins that they commit. *That* they commit sins is, however, an inevitable consequence of their living a life defined (in part at least) by sin.

Yet, however rooted in human nature sin may be, it cannot be natural and still be sin. Sin is, necessarily, a distortion of what ought to be, and Paul believes that people remain aware, at some level, of the wrongfulness of much of what they do, and desire, at some level, to do better. In this sense there is within human beings an "I" that recognizes goodness and longs to embrace it. Yet such is the hold of sin upon people's lives that they cannot yield the truly good more than fitful acknowledgment. They are sin's slaves—paradoxically, both *with* their will (they *choose* to do what they should not do) and *without* it (they nonetheless recognize and regret the wrong in what they do). So Paul depicts the disordered personality of Adamic humanity.[12]

---

8. Romans 5:12.

9. Romans 1:18–21.

10. The "many" of whom Paul speaks in this verse are all Adam's descendants, or all humankind.

11. Romans 6:1–2.

12. In this paragraph I have drawn on Romans 7:15–24. Some interpreters, however, think that this passage has in view the continued moral struggles of the Christian. They think it unlikely that Paul would attribute to Adamic humanity a desire for what is good. I (with many other interpreters) find it more improbable that Paul could depict Christian existence as one of being "sold under sin" (Romans 7:14; contrast Romans 6:18, 22), powerless to deal with the "flesh" (Romans 7:18; contrast Romans 8:9), engaged in a struggle with sin in which God's Spirit plays no evident part (note the absence of any reference to God's Spirit in 7:15–24; and contrast Romans 8:3–4, 9). See further chapter 9, below.

How are we to understand Paul's notion of a sin*fulness* that is prior to particular sins? That is rooted and universal in human nature while remaining a distortion of what ought to be? That enslaves its subjects? Whenever people deliberately choose not to do what (at some level) they acknowledge ought to be done, and whenever people deliberately choose to do what (at some level) they acknowledge ought not to be done, more is involved than their succumbing to the lure of a particular temptation. They are expressing the priority they give to their own choosing over their respect for what is right and good. In effect, they are staking out a claim to be gods themselves, to determine good and evil for themselves. These are *moral* choices, choices that (according to the "Jewish-Christian" worldview) are wrongly made. And certainly we can imagine created, intelligent beings (such as the angels who serve God in the biblical tradition) who choose differently. Yet such choices *are* made and have been made throughout human history. Humanity is marked by its insistence on choosing its own course of action *and* by the expression of this insistence in deeds it knows to be wrong.

At some point some human being or beings with sufficient grasp of the options before them must have been the first to make a morally *wrong* choice. But the human condition (Paul believes) is not now what it was then. The orientation adopted by those who first committed sin seems now a fixture in human nature. The self-absorption, the insistence on self-rule, the lack of faith in God that take expression in particular sins are all part and parcel of the human condition. Yet (and this is essential) they are just as wrong, and just as much a distortion of the way humans were meant to live, as ever. However common deceit, jealousy, strife, and violence may be, they remain sin, and the world in which they occur is not the world as it ought to be. Humans still owe God the wholehearted trust and obedience due his goodness—though, slaves of sin that they are, they are both unable and unwilling to give it.[13] Sin "dwells" in them.[14] It dogs them even when they feel a desire to do the good.[15] If it seems dormant for a time, it leaps to resistance when it encounters a

13. Romans 8:7–8.
14. Romans 7:17.
15. Romans 7:21.

divine commandment.[16] Apart from a divine transformation, humanity's bent for sin is incorrigible.

Can Adamic humanity do anything good? Yes, Paul would say—and no. Paul recognizes (as we have seen) that people have moral sensibilities, and he does not deny that they sometimes act in accordance with these sensibilities.[17] On the other hand, he believes that sin has taken radical root in human nature. The blunt truth of the matter, as Paul sees it, seems to be this: people do much that would be both good and God-pleasing *if* it were done as an expression of their wholehearted faith in God. Yet even such deeds cannot, finally, be either God-pleasing or good when they represent behavior adopted by a self that, at its deepest roots, is determined to pursue its own goals: "Whatever is not an expression of faith is sin."[18]

The Rule of Death

With sin comes death: for Paul,[19] Genesis,[20] and biblical tradition as a whole, the two belong together. Greed, anger, malice, lust, and the like are seen as sins against life as God meant it to be. They disfigure the innocence of creation and wreak havoc and death within it.[21] God will not sustain forever the life of those who choose to live independently of him and in defiance of love; nor will he give them forever to mar his handiwork. The soul that sins, dies.[22] Indeed, the whole created order sullied by sin has been subjected to decay and death.[23] Were it to continue forever in its disfigured state, the Creator's designs for its goodness would be foiled.

16. Romans 7:8–9.
17. For Paul's recognition of pagan moral sensibilities, see, in addition to Romans 2, Romans 12:17; 14:18; 1 Corinthians 5:1; 2 Corinthians 8:21.
18. Romans 14:23. The principle seems true to Paul, even though its original application in Romans 14 is more limited. A similar perspective is apparent in the well-known words of Jesus in Matthew 7:17–18: "Thus every good tree yields good fruit, whereas every rotten tree yields bad fruit. A good tree cannot yield bad fruit, nor can a rotten tree yield good."
19. Romans 5:12; 6:23.
20. Genesis 2:17.
21. See, most graphically, Genesis 6:11–13.
22. Ezekiel 18:4.
23. Romans 8:20.

Nor, in biblical terminology, is the death linked to sin merely physical. Indeed in the Hebrew Scriptures, physical death is not always regarded as an evil: not, for example, when a patriarch dies "in a good old age, . . . full of years,"[24] particularly if he has been able to bounce great-grandchildren on his knees.[25] Still, death brings an end to the activities and relationships one has known, even—as the psalmists are wont to point out—to the joy of praising God.[26] Moreover, death is said to cast its shadow over the still living when disease or distress prevents them from knowing the cheers of normal human existence.[27] In such cases we may speak of a kind of spiritual death. To be delivered from such distress is spoken of as an escape from death, and the psalmists who know such deliverance are exuberant in their praise of the divine Life-Giver.[28]

The psalmists' relish for life is clearly rooted in their sense of being at home in an ordered, benevolent cosmos. They acknowledge that it is God who has "made us, and not we ourselves,"[29] that "we are his people, and the sheep of his pasture," that he is "good" and worthy of trust and praise.[30] To refuse God recognition is to quit the cosmic dance, to make do on one's own in a world whose goodness is a gift of love to be celebrated with all God's creatures.[31] The psalmists see nothing admirable or splendid in those who choose the path of isolation: only self-absorption,[32]

> My vows to you I must perform,
>   O God;
>   I will render thank offerings
>   to you.
> For you have delivered my soul
>   from death,
>   and my feet from falling,
> so that I may walk before God
>   in the light of life.
>
> Psalm 56:12–13 NRSV

---

24. Genesis 25:8.
25. Genesis 50:23.
26. See Psalm 6:5; 88:10–12; 115:17; Isaiah 38:18. In chapter 4 I noted that belief in a vital afterlife is not found in much of the Hebrew Bible.
27. Psalm 18:4–5; 31:9–13; 88:3–18.
28. Psalm 116:1–19; see also Psalm 9:13–14; 56:10–13; Isaiah 38:15–20.
29. Or "made us, and his we are."
30. Psalm 100 KJV.
31. See, for example, Psalm 148.
32. Psalm 10:4; 12:3–4.

mulish stubbornness,[33] incredible folly,[34] a slippery pathway,[35] and certain doom.[36] Nor is death only a fate that awaits them; already they have cut themselves off from life as it was meant to be lived.[37]

In short, when Paul wrote, "The wages of sin is death,"[38] he was merely giving epigrammatic expression to a principle that, according to the "Jewish-Christian" worldview, is basic to life.

To sum up these principles of life, as Paul sees them:

1. Humans were made to enjoy a privileged position in a world created good.
2. Through their refusal to acknowledge and trust God, and their determination to pursue their own (self-defined) good, humans have fallen from the "glory" for which God intended them.[39]
3. Such was the choice of Adam. His sin marked out the boundaries within which humanity now lives. People choose, commit, and are responsible for their own individual sins. In so doing, however, they are merely giving personal expression to the will for self-rule that characterizes the whole human race.
4. Humans retain enough of a sense of the good to know that they have sinned against it, and indeed desire, at some level, to do what is right. Their sin thus remains a sin against the truth, a living lie that destroys the sinner's integrity.
5. Sin kills.

A New Human Prototype

Jesus Christ was (1) a man of a different ilk, (2) introduced by God (3) into Adamic humanity (4) to offset the sin of Adam and (5) to liberate Adam's offspring from the tyranny of sin and death.

33. Psalm 32:9.
34. Psalm 14:1; 94:6–11.
35. Psalm 73:18.
36. Psalm 37:12–13, 20, 35–36, 38.
37. See Psalm 32:3–4.
38. Romans 6:23.
39. Romans 3:23.

Those who belong to Christ (6) enjoy freedom from sin's rule, though they (7) must practice this freedom to maintain it.

1. As we saw in the last chapter, Jesus was, for Paul, more than a man: he was God's "Son" sent in human "flesh" like our "sinful flesh" to condemn and conquer sin.[40] That he was God's Son accounts for his ability (not otherwise found in Adamic humanity) to overcome sin and live a life marked by radical trust and obedience toward God.[41] But such—it must be remembered—was the life for which all humanity was intended; it needed, therefore, to be lived by one who was human if the divine purposes for humanity were to be realized. God's Son though he was, Christ was also, and needed to be, a man in order to counter the sin of the man Adam and restore Adam's descendants to the life humans were made to enjoy.

> For since death came through a man, through a man came also the resurrection of the dead. For as in Adam all die, so in Christ all will be made alive.[42]

2. The life and death of Christ as a man, and the possibility he procured for humanity to be delivered from sin and restored to God's favor, are all gifts of God's grace. Paul does not begrudge the ink required to underline the point.[43]

3. Humanity apart from Christ is "in Adam," living in conditions determined by Adam's sin: slaves themselves of sin, cut off from God's favor, subject to condemnation and death. Jesus lived in a body and under conditions like those under which other humans sin.

> But the free gift is not like the trespass. For if the many died through the one man's trespass, much more surely have the grace of God and the free gift in the grace of the one man, Jesus Christ, abounded for the many.
>
> Romans 5:15 NRSV

4. Christ, however, obeyed God throughout (and, in the end, at the cost of) his life. He thus, "in the flesh," overcame and

40. Romans 8:3.
41. See Romans 5:19.
42. First Corinthians 15:21–22.
43. Romans 5:15–21.

condemned the "sin in the flesh" to which other human beings succumb:[44] such sin, in this case, is a defeated power. Having died, he left the sphere over which sin exercises its tyranny. Having risen again, he lives for God, no longer encumbered by the weaknesses and temptations to which humanity on a sin-scarred earth is inevitably subject.[45] It behooves humanity to somehow be detached from the conditions of life that resulted from Adam's disobedience and to share the possibilities of a different life opened up by Christ's obedience.

> The death he died, he died to sin, once for all; but the life he lives, he lives to God. So you also must consider yourselves dead to sin and alive to God in Christ Jesus.
>
> Romans 6:10–11 NRSV

5. God refuses to abandon his creatures to the power of evil. His purpose is to rescue humanity through Christ. To accomplish this end, he has ordained that Adamic human beings can be "united with Christ." Their baptism marks them out as those who, with Jesus, have died to the life that was marred by sin[46] and now share with Christ a new life in God's service.[47] The baptized are no longer "Adam-people" but, by a divine transference, "Christ-people," members of the new humanity,[48] whose terms of existence are defined, not by Adam's disobedience, but by the obedience and righteousness of Christ.

> Do you not know that all of us who have been baptized into Christ Jesus were baptized into his death? Therefore we have been buried with him by baptism into death, so that, just as Christ was raised from the dead by the glory of the Father, so we too might walk in newness of life.
>
> Romans 6:3–4 NRSV

44. Romans 8:3.
45. Romans 6:10.
46. For the notion, see, in addition to Romans 6, Galatians 2:19–20; 5:24; 6:14; also 2 Corinthians 4:10. The implication, of course, is that Adamic humanity cannot be fitted for God's kingdom by adjustments here and improvements there. To prescribe repentance and new resolutions is no remedy. The self that is corrupted by sin must die and in its place new life be given (by God, of course; see Romans 4:17).
47. Romans 6:3–11.
48. See also 2 Corinthians 5:17.

6. Those who, with Christ, have "died to sin" have been set free from its tyranny.[49] While they clung to their self-rule and self-absorption, they could not lose themselves in God's love, embrace and delight in his goodness, or know the sense of "belonging" in a cosmos steered by his benevolence. From such a life of goodness, Paul says (with deliberate irony), they were then completely "free."[50] Now that they have died to sin, however, they enjoy a new—and true—freedom, empowered by the Spirit of Christ, with countless possibilities of service and celebration to be explored throughout life—here and beyond the grave.[51]

7. But the earthly life of believers has an in-between character. Believers have died—with Christ—to sin; they have been set free from the lie of their independence and their insistence on self-rule. They are assured of life—with Christ—and have already experienced the presence of the Holy Spirit as a power for good and a foretaste of divine favors still to come. Nonetheless, they continue to live in a body exposed to the temptations of sin. And though they are not likely to renounce the new life for the old, there is a risk that they will try to combine the two. Can one not (they may suppose) "continue in sin," not out of defiance toward God, but—on the contrary—trusting in his unlimited grace?[52]

Such a marriage of heaven and hell is not an option. Sin enslaves and leads to death. Goodness and life in God's service are open only to those who have renounced self-rule, who have "died" to sin: for them continued acquiescence in its thralldom is inconceivable.[53] That believers struggle with temptation is

> What then are we to say? Should we continue in sin in order that grace may abound? By no means! How can we who died to sin go on living in it? . . . Do you not know that if you present yourselves to anyone as obedient slaves, you are slaves of the one whom you obey, either of sin, which leads to death, or of obedience, which leads to righteousness?
>
> Romans 6:1–2, 16 NRSV

---

49. Romans 6:7, 10–11, 18, 22.
50. Romans 6:20.
51. Romans 7:6; 8:9–11.
52. Romans 6:1.
53. Romans 6:2.

presupposed throughout Romans 6. That they can succumb to its lure, be "overtaken" by particular sins, and need restoration was an experience with which Paul was clearly familiar.[54] That becoming like Christ is a transformation taking place (not without stops and starts, falls and new beginnings) over a lifetime[55] and more is self-evident.[56] But would-be believers cannot reembrace the lie of their own independence or give themselves to the pursuit of sin without losing the freedom they now claim to enjoy.[57]

---

54. Galatians 6:1; 1 Corinthians 10:13.
55. Second Corinthians 3:18.
56. Philippians 3:20–21.
57. Romans 6:16.

9

The Goals and Goodness
of the Law

Romans 7:1–8:13

Pablo Casals used to decry the "bad German tradition" that treated Johann Sebastian Bach as Herr Professor and regarded his unaccompanied cello suites as nothing more than musical exercises. Casals himself brought a passion to their performance that opened the eyes of many to their awesome power: the power of the "terrifying Bach,"[1] of Bach the "volcano"—whom "purists" would reduce to a professor![2]

Paul's letters are no less dynamic than Bach's cello suites; yet Paul, no less than Bach, is in need of a Pablo Casals to rescue him from the awful clutches of those who would make him a *professor*. Dispassionate reconstructions of Paul's views of sin, of Christ's love, of "redemption" and "salvation," can hardly breed an understanding of Paul or make his impact comprehensible.

1. So Casals quotes Mendelssohn—with approval.
2. References are taken from "Casals: A Living Portrait," a Columbia Masterworks recording (no date given).

"Paul and the law" has become a topic for academic debate. For Paul, the law was anything but an academic matter. We begin by asking why.

> With my whole heart I seek you;
>   do not let me stray from your
>   commandments.
> I treasure your word in my heart,
>   so that I may not sin against
>   you.
> Blessed are you, O LORD;
>   teach me your statutes.
> With my lips I declare
>   all the ordinances of your
>   mouth.
> I delight in the way of your
>   decrees
>   as much as in all riches.
> I will meditate on your precepts,
>   and fix my eyes on your ways.
> I will delight in your statutes;
>   I will not forget your word.
> Deal bountifully with your
>   servant,
>   so that I may live and observe
>   your word.
> Open my eyes, so that I may
>   behold
>   wondrous things out of your
>   law.
>
> Psalm 119:10–18 NRSV

God of Moses—God of Christ Jesus

For Paul, the law was "holy," its "commandment holy, righteous, and good."[3] The terms permit definition, but Paul's point can scarcely be grasped from within the disenchanted horizons of our day. If, for us, the world is purely material, its order no more than mechanical, then—to understand Paul—we need to recapture the vision of a cosmos fashioned and steered by divine goodness, and of human beings as a vital part of its order. That the law is holy then means that it comes from the God who made and sustains us—together with all his creation. That its demands are righteous and good means that those who keep them will be in tune with reality: this is the way we *ought* to live in the world as God has made it. That God gave the law to Israel must be reckoned among the greatest proofs of his love.[4]

Sympathetic readers of Psalm 119 will grasp something of the treasured place occupied by torah[5] for those whose horizons

---

3. Romans 7:12.

4. Romans 3:1–2; 9:4; and compare Psalm 147:19–20.

5. The term *torah* here refers to the sum of commands and prohibitions, with the accompanying blessings (for obedience) and curses (for disobedience), that God gave to Israel at Mount Sinai. See chapter 4, above.

included the holy and the good and who saw torah's laws as their embodiment.

Paul was certainly among them. Before his adoption of the Christian cause, he excelled his contemporaries in his devotion to the law.[6] Nor did his coming to Christian faith do anything to alter his convictions about the sacredness of torah's demands. On the contrary: it was essential to Paul's understanding of Christ that his death expressed the love for sinners of the same God who created them and whose benevolent will was expressed in the law that they had defied. The God of Christ Jesus was also the God of Moses: but Sinai could no longer be seen as the locus of God's *decisive* revelation.

In Deuteronomy (as we have seen), Israel's enjoyment of life and divine blessing depended on the people's obedience to the will of God revealed in the torah.[7] For Paul (as we have also seen), enjoyment of life and divine blessing depended on faith in Christ.[8] The latter conviction—forced upon Paul, he believed, by a personal revelation of God's Son—required Paul to reevaluate the place of torah in the divine agenda. In what follows I will attempt to summarize the results of his reevaluation.

The Righteousness of the Law

Paul remained convinced that torah had been divinely given; indeed, God had displayed his glory when he had made known his laws.[9] If given by God, then torah's demands *must* be "holy, righteous, and good"—and God must have had a reason for giving them.

Though all of torah's commands were "righteous" and "good," their righteousness and goodness were of different kinds.[10] Paul does not draw explicit distinctions in his writings. Nonetheless, when he speaks of Gentiles who keep the law, or of the law's

6. Such, to be sure, is his own claim (Galatians 1:14); but the passion and single-mindedness he brought to his Christian apostleship leave no reason to doubt his self-perception on this point.

7. See chapter 4, above.

8. See chapter 6, above.

9. Second Corinthians 3:7.

10. See the discussion on "The Place of Law in Deuteronomy" in chapter 4, above.

requirements as "written" on Gentile "hearts" and attested by their "conscience,"[11] he is clearly referring to the moral demands of the Mosaic law: Gentiles, too, know that it is wrong to murder, commit adultery, steal. It is clear that Paul did *not* think that Gentiles were aware of, or subject to, an obligation to keep Israel's food or festival laws. The same exclusive focus on the law's *moral* demands may well be present when Paul says that Christians are enabled by God's Spirit to fulfill "the righteous demand of the law,"[12] and that "love is the fulfilling of the law."[13] The moral demands of the law are "righteous" and "good" because they spell out what behavior is appropriate for all human beings living in God's world.

But the law also contains commands about circumcision, festival observances, and permitted and forbidden foods: Paul insisted that these commands were *not* to be imposed on Gentiles even when Gentiles become members (together with Jewish Christians) in the new people of God. The righteousness and goodness of such demands[14] lay in the opportunity they gave Jews to trust and obey God in all areas of their lives. These commands, however, were given *only* to Jews. In Paul's view (shared by many Jews), it was neither in their nature nor in God's purpose that they should be universalized.

The Weakness of the Law

The Israel to whom the law was given belonged to Adamic humanity. Favored though it was, Israel continued to be marked by the Adamic refusal to trust God and submit to his will. In Pauline terminology, the law encountered, and could not overcome, the "flesh."

11. Romans 2:14–15, 26–27.
12. Romans 8:4. Alternatively, the "righteous demand" (singular) of the law may be for that faith and obedience toward God implicit in all of the law's particular demands.
13. Romans 13:8–10; compare Galatians 5:14. Note, in Romans 13:9, that it is moral demands that are cited as "summed up" in the love command.
14. Paul himself does not address this issue. The view here summarized was standard among Jews. Allegorical interpretations of such laws were also common among Jews of Paul's day (forbidden foods, for example, might be seen as symbols of various vices). The latter interpretations, of course, ran the risk of undercutting the importance of literal observance of the law.

Paul can speak of life "in the flesh" in a neutral way, meaning life as we know it (life lived "in the body").[15] But since such life in the flesh is marked by humanity's resistance to God, Paul can also use the word "flesh" to refer to humanity's bent for sin:[16] nothing good lives in the "flesh";[17] the "flesh" is at war with God's Spirit;[18] it does not, and cannot, submit to God's law.[19] "Those who are in the flesh cannot please God."[20]

Paul dramatizes the encounter between God's law and the flesh in Romans 7:7–13, then explains its outcome in 7:14–25. Though he speaks in the first person of what "I" have experienced, the account is intended to be generic, not strictly autobiographical: Paul wants to clarify the role played by the law in humanity's enslavement to sin while nonetheless maintaining that the law itself is good.[21] Throughout the section, the "I" is a creature of flesh whose horizons are defined by the sinful orientation of Adamic humanity. For a time, perhaps, the sin that insists on self-rule and refuses to trust and submit to God may lie dormant ("dead," in the terminology of Romans 7:8): for just so long, that is, as the "I" does not find itself confronted with a divine command. When such a confrontation takes place, however, a disastrous outcome is inevitable.

Not that the law is responsible—far from it! There is nothing wrong (Paul insists) with the law or its commands. If rightly embraced in a spirit of trust and obedience, they would lead to life.[22] Such, however, is not the mind-set of Adamic humanity. Its innate rebelliousness and insistence on self-rule spring to life when God (by giving the law) demands its obedience.[23] Whatever

15. Romans 9:3, 5; Galatians 2:20.
16. Note Paul's play on the two senses of "flesh" in 2 Corinthians 10:3.
17. Romans 7:18.
18. Galatians 5:17.
19. Romans 8:7.
20. Romans 8:8.
21. Note the questions that Paul is attempting to answer in Romans 7:7, 13. His statement in Romans 7:9–10 in particular is hard to explain as strictly autobiographical. The discrepancy between, on the one hand, the utter despair of ever doing the good that the "I" of Romans 7:15–25 exhibits and, on the other hand, Paul's own "robust conscience" as exhibited in Philippians 3:4–6 is also frequently cited as evidence that the former description is not primarily autobiographical.
22. Romans 7:10.
23. Romans 7:7–11.

lingering awareness sinful human beings may have of a good that they have not themselves defined, whatever yearning they may feel to pursue it, in the end it is sin that rules the day.[24] The commandment, the observance of which would bring life, is transgressed. The result is death.[25]

Such an understanding of what happens when God's law meets the sinful flesh underlies other claims in Paul's writings about what happened to Israel after God entrusted it with the

> What then should we say? That the law is sin? By no means! Yet, if it had not been for the law, I would not have known sin. I would not have known what it is to covet if the law had not said, "You shall not covet." But sin, seizing an opportunity in the commandment, produced in me all kinds of covetousness. Apart from the law sin lies dead. I was once alive apart from the law, but when the commandment came, sin revived and I died, and the very commandment that promised life proved to be death to me. For sin, seizing an opportunity in the commandment, deceived me and through it killed me. So the law is holy, and the commandment is holy and just and good.
>
> Did what is good, then, bring death to me? By no means! It was sin, working death in me through what is good, in order that sin might be shown to be sin, and through the commandment might become sinful beyond measure.
>
> For we know that the law is spiritual; but I am of the flesh, sold into slavery under sin.
>
> Romans 7:7–14 NRSV

law. Paul concludes his portrayal of humanity's sin[26] with the claim that those to whom the law was given have gone astray from God no less than have the Gentiles. The giving of the law has thus resulted, not in a vital relationship between Israel and God, but in an indictment of *universal* human sinfulness.[27] Else-

24. Romans 7:15–25.
25. Romans 7:10.
26. Romans 1:18–3:20.
27. Romans 3:19–20.

where Paul speaks of the law and the covenant of which it is a part as bringing divine wrath,[28] a divine curse,[29] condemnation, and death.[30] The assumption throughout is that even the most favored segment of Adamic humanity—God's chosen people, Israel—rebels against God. By breaking God's law, Israel has brought upon itself the "death" with which the law threatens its transgressors.[31]

What led Paul to so pessimistic a judgment? Three factors are key.

1. The first and ultimately decisive factor must have been the Christian belief that salvation was to be found in Christ, who had died for the sins of humanity.[32] From such a conviction (which Paul adopted after his Damascus-road encounter with Christ), two things followed. First, even though the law promises life to those who keep its demands, *that* path to life must no longer be open; otherwise there would be no reason for God now to offer salvation in Christ. Second, the dilemma from which Christ saves has been brought about by human sin.

2. If God has provided Christ to save people from their sins, then people are sinners and the law cannot save them: Paul's understanding of the human problem was worked out in the light of what he believed to be God's solution. But he found *confirmation* for this view in the venerable Jewish tradition that saw Israel's waywardness as no less incorrigible than Gentile vice. The history of Israel as related in its Scriptures was a sorry litany of unfaithfulness and rebellion. Israel's prophets told a similar tale. There was thus nothing new in Paul's view that Israel had rejected God's law and proved no more righteous than the Gentiles.

3. To revelation and tradition we should certainly add observation as a third factor in Paul's judgment. Romans 7:7–25 is not primarily autobiographical; yet it seems most unlikely that Paul had no personal experience of the dilemma he there

28. Romans 4:15.
29. Galatians 3:10, 13.
30. Second Corinthians 3:7, 9.
31. See also Romans 5:13, 20; 7:5; 8:2; 1 Corinthians 15:56.
32. Notice how, in 1 Corinthians 15:3, Paul sums up the gospel that *he himself received* and that he had preached to others: "Christ *died* for our *sins* . . ."

describes in the first person. No doubt his Christian convictions have colored his depiction of the inability of the sinful "I" to do the good. But he can hardly have been exempt from the widely attested sense of frustration that accompanies serious moral effort—particularly when he has himself provided as graphic an account of it as any. Even with the best of intentions (Paul must have judged from his own experience), human beings fall short of the goodness that they know they ought to show.[33]

> I do not understand my own actions. For I do not do what I want, but I do the very thing I hate. . . . I know that nothing good dwells within me, that is, in my flesh. I can will what is right, but I cannot do it. . . .
>
> So I find it to be a law that when I want to do what is good, evil lies close at hand. For I delight in the law of God in my inmost self, but I see in my members another law at war with the law of my mind, making me captive to the law of sin that dwells in my members. Wretched man that I am! Who will rescue me from this body of death? Thanks be to God through Jesus Christ our Lord!
>
> Romans 7:15–25 NRSV

Thus, when Paul needs to explain why the gift of the divine law has not brought life as it promises, he says simply that those subject to the law have not met its conditions, its demands for obedience. Romans 3:27–30 suggests, however, two additional reasons why observance of the law could not have been the divinely intended means for people to secure good relations with God.

The second of these reasons is not controversial—at least with regard to our understanding of Paul's point. The law was given to Jews. But God is not the God of Jews only. One would expect the God of all the earth to open a path to fellowship with himself

33. Philippians 3:6 does not rule out such a reading of Paul. The text is not in any case a claim to sinless perfection, but only to a serious attempt to observe the law, including its prescribed rites of atonement for shortcomings. Adherents of the "righteousness under the law" would have counted such an attempt as passing muster (hence "blameless"). Note too, however, that Paul is here bent on undercutting the pretensions to faithful observance of the law of people whose zeal in no way (he believed) approximated his own. The argument calls for evidence of Paul's erstwhile devotion to the law; it need not exclude an experience of moral struggle such as that attested in Romans 7.

that puts all peoples on an equal footing. Such is the path, not of the law, but of faith.[34]

The first reason is that a law that demands deeds leaves open the door for human boasting—and Paul believes that human boasting before God is inappropriate.[35] Controversy surrounds the type of boasting Paul has in mind. Is he thinking of Jews who boast that they must be special because God has given them his law? Or is he thinking of people boasting because they think that they have *kept* the law and so secured a place in God's favor? In support of the former interpretation we may point to the Jewish boasting mentioned in Romans 2:17, where the focus of the boast is on the divine privileges granted to Israel. But the second interpretation seems stronger. Paul notes in Romans 3:27 that while boasting is invited by a law that demands "works," it is excluded if the pathway to divine favor is that of faith.[36] He picks up the same point at the beginning of chapter 4: Abraham would have been entitled to boast if God had approved him because of his works. Such approval, after all, would have represented, not a gift of God's grace, but God's recognition of Abraham's achievement. In reality, however, God's approval of Abraham was not a reward for what Abraham had done but an act of his own divine grace—as it must be *whenever* God declares guilty people (the "ungodly") who believe to be innocent (or

> Then what becomes of boasting? It is excluded. By what law? By that of works? No, but by the law of faith. For we hold that a person is justified by faith apart from works prescribed by the law. Or is God the God of Jews only? Is he not the God of Gentiles also? Yes, of Gentiles also, since God is one; and he will justify the circumcised on the ground of faith and the uncircumcised through that same faith.
>
> Romans 3:27–30 NRSV

---

34. Romans 3:29–30.

35. Romans 3:27–28; compare 1 Corinthians 1:26–31; Galatians 6:14.

36. The "law of faith" in this verse means the "principle of faith": Paul is playing with different senses of the word *law*. Some interpreters do take the "law of faith" to be a reference to the Mosaic law, noting that the demand that underlies all of its particular demands is for faith in God. It seems unlikely, however, that Paul is making such a point in this passage, since here he repeatedly *contrasts* the "law" (or the "works of the law") with "faith" (Romans 3:21–22, 28, 31; 4:13–14).

"righteous"). Here it is clear that Paul regards the path of faith, of complete dependence on God, as one that rules out boasting in human achievement. It is also clear, however, that *any* path involving human works (and that necessarily includes the path of the law, with its demand for proper works) *invites* boasting. Paul's sense of the appropriate stance of humans before God, then, requires that faith, not works, be the principle by which humans enjoy good relations with their Maker.[37]

Why, Then, the Law?

So far Paul's logic seems straightforward enough. God expects people to do what is right and good. He gave the people of Israel his law so that what they were supposed to do would be perfectly clear. Ever since Adam, however, it is in the nature of human beings not to want to be *told* what to do. And ever since Adam, people have chosen to do much that they know is neither right nor good. The people of Israel are no exception: they have persistently broken God's law. As a result, humans have caused themselves no end of trouble; and the law, for all the rightness and goodness of its demands, is *not* the way to get them out of it.

At this point, however, we may want to ask Paul a different question. God must have known what would happen when he gave people his law. Since they have not obeyed it, why did he bother?

Perhaps we need, first, to note again Paul's insistence that the law was a gift of God's goodness and a peculiar favor entrusted to Israel.[38] That Jews did not *obey* the law in no way alters its character as "holy," or that of its commands as "holy, righteous, and good."[39] There is a holiness, a rightness, and a goodness in

---

37. Compare Ephesians 2:8–9. (Note, however, that scholars debate whether Ephesians was written by Paul or by someone close to him writing in his name.) The reluctance to see Paul as concerned about boasting in one's observance of the law appears to me to be largely rooted in a commendable desire to undercut a stereotypical depiction of Jews as self-righteous and boastful. It should be emphasized that Paul does not appear to regard Jews as distinguished by a propensity to boasting peculiar to themselves. *Any* boasting of the "flesh" (that is, of Adamic humanity) before God he finds inappropriate.

38. Romans 3:1–2; 9:3–4.

39. Romans 3:2–3; 7:12.

stating the truth about humans and their place in God's world that is not affected by their response.[40]

But it is also (Paul would say) good that the law identified sin as such and condemned it. Sin was present in the world and worked its deadly bane throughout the period from Adam to Moses, even before the law was given:[41] murder, adultery, and theft did not first become wrong when God included them in the list of things that Israel was not supposed to do. But the giving of the law served to mark out such sins as *transgressions:* as the willful violation of identifiable, recognized, and legitimate demands.[42] Deeds wrong in any case now represented the deliberate flouting of God's commands.[43] Indeed (as noted earlier in this chapter), when the rebellious "flesh" encountered God's law, its inchoate rebelliousness acquired a focus against which it could direct its defiance, and sin multiplied.[44] Not that the spread of sin is a good thing; but the recognition[45] and indictment[46] of humanity's rebelliousness *are* good, even *necessary* steps in the ultimate banishment of all that corrupts the goodness of God's creation.[47]

> Now we know that whatever the law says, it speaks to those who are under the law, so that every mouth may be silenced, and the whole world may be held accountable to God. For "no human being will be justified in his sight" by deeds prescribed by the law, for through the law comes the knowledge of sin.
>
> Romans 3:19–20 NRSV

40. For a similar sentiment, see Ezekiel 2:3–5.

41. Romans 5:13–14.

42. Romans 4:15.

43. To illustrate the point: In Jason's household it is considered wrong for him to help himself to cookies without asking. The defiance involved in such an act is multiplied, however, if he has just been told that the freshly baked cookies on the table have been made for a party and must not be touched. In particular periods of childhood rebelliousness, such a recognized opportunity to defy a parent's edict may in fact be more determinative of Jason's conduct than the lure of the chocolate chips in the cookies.

44. Romans 5:20; 7:5, 7–13.

45. Romans 3:20; 7:7.

46. Romans 4:15.

47. Paul would also have shared the early Christian conviction that Israel's sacrificial cult as ordained in torah served the positive function of foreshadow-

The Fulfillment of the Law

Paul is adamant that the law's demand of circumcision is
not to be imposed on Gentile believers.[48] He declares that the
period of the law's validity ended with the coming of Christ.[49]
He claims in various ways that believers are no longer subject
to the commands and sanctions of the law: they have "died to
the law";[50] they have been "set free" from the law;[51] they are no
longer "under" the law;[52] they have been "redeemed" from its
sway.[53] All of this would be perfectly straightforward were it not
also clear that Paul expected Christian behavior to comply with
the moral demands of the law.[54] Indeed, his letters are remark-
ably well stocked with prescriptions for believers' behavior, many
of them no different from the demands of the Mosaic law. Not
surprisingly, a number of scholars have announced a breakdown
in apostolic logic at this point.

Others have rushed to the apostle's defense with a distinction
that would preserve his consistency: Paul believed, they suggest,
that Christians were no longer bound by the *ritual* or *ceremonial*
demands of the law (for example, those involving circumcision,
food, and festival observances), though they were still subject to
its *moral* commands. The suggestion is both simple and plau-
sible, and may claim as support those passages in which Paul
speaks simply of "the law" while intending only its moral com-
ponent.[55] Perhaps it is the best that we can make of a complex
point in Paul's writings. To my mind, however, neither the charge

ing (providing an interpretive framework for understanding the significance of)
Christ's death. See the discussion of "Early Christian Perspectives," in chapter
5, above. When Paul asks why the law was given, however, he has in mind its
moral demands (see Romans 3:20; 5:20; Galatians 3:19).

48. Paul's letter to the Galatians was written to make this point. It is also
reflected in Romans 4:9–17.

49. Galatians 3:19, 23–25; see 2 Corinthians 3:11, 14. Romans 10:4 makes
the same point if Paul here means by the Greek word *telos* "end" and not simply
"goal."

50. Romans 7:6; Galatians 2:19.

51. Romans 7:6.

52. Romans 6:14–15.

53. Galatians 4:5.

54. See Romans 8:4; 13:8–10; Galatians 5:14.

55. Note especially Romans 2:14–27.

of inconsistency nor the defense that limits Christian freedom from the law to an exemption from its ritual demands[56] does justice to an important Pauline theme.

Romans 7:5–6 provides the key. For those who are "in the flesh" (that is, for those who are not inclined to submit to God's will), an encounter with the law (that tells them what God wants them to do) rouses "sinful passions," leading to acts of rebellion and death. The demands that incite such rebellion can hardly be exclusively ceremonial; on the contrary, the example Paul provides in verse 7 is the (moral) prohibition of coveting for oneself what belongs to others. Yet in the preceding verse Paul says that believers have been set free ("discharged") from the law (the context forbids us to limit the latter statement to the law's *ritual* aspects), so that they now serve God in the new way of the Spirit rather than the old way of the "written code" (literally, the "letter").

> While we were living in the flesh, our sinful passions, aroused by the law, were at work in our members to bear fruit for death. But now we are discharged from the law, dead to that which held us captive, so that we are slaves not under the old written code but in the new life of the Spirit.
>
> Romans 7:5–6 NRSV

There is no question (could there ever be?) that Christians are bound to serve God. Nor is there (for Paul) any question that believers, as dwellers in God's world, are subject to precisely the same universal obligations of truth, goodness, and love that are spelled out in the moral demands of the Mosaic law. Indeed, when they live as they ought and as God's Spirit enables them, their conduct will prove unexceptionable by the standards of the law.[57] Paul's point is simply that believers do not encounter these obligations as *law*.

"Law," in this Pauline usage, stands not simply for the concrete commands and prohibitions found in torah, but also for the way in which these obligations encounter rebellious humanity: those "in the flesh," bent on doing as *they* please, can only experience

---

56. Everyone, of course, agrees that Paul also means that Christians have been delivered from the curse that the law pronounces against those who transgress it. See Galatians 3:13.

57. Galatians 5:22–23.

God's law as an unwanted imposition.[58] When God gave Israel the law, Israel served as a representative part of the humanity that God was *preparing* for restoration to its intended place in his creation; it was a humanity that had not yet "come of age."[59] In giving the law, God provided his wayward creatures with a fitting and graphic reminder that he is good, that human beings have been made to enjoy fellowship with him, and that that fellowship requires their own submission to the good. Inevitably, however, the latter requirement could only encounter Adamic humanity as (unwanted) *law*.

But law (in this sense) is a matter of the past for a humanity that has "come of age." Its ceremonial aspects were never intended for any but Jews. Even its moral demands now have a different character. To be sure, murder, adultery, and theft are as wrong for Christians as they ever were for Israel under the law. Moreover, so long as Christians are subject to the weakness and temptations of life in a sin-scarred world, they will need guidance (or, at least, reminders) about which kinds of conduct are appropriate and which kinds are inappropriate and wrong for them to exhibit. We may go further. There is, in Paul's understanding, a continuing place for figures of authority in the church to provide such guidance and, if necessary, to insist upon its obligatory nature. Paul himself does not hesitate to advise, to remind, to command. But even where he commands, he insists that he is merely spelling out what is implicit in his Christian readers' own faith and experience of God.[60] Appropriate behavior for believers is, for Paul, the natural expression of their trust in God and their experience of his indwelling Spirit.[61] They have "crucified the flesh."[62] No longer can God's will confront them as an arbitrary, vexing, and provocative *law*.

58. Note how Paul links the spheres of the Mosaic law and the "flesh" in Romans 7:5–6, 14–24; Galatians 3:2–3; Philippians 3:3–4, 9.
59. Galatians 3:23–26; 4:1–7.
60. See Romans 15:14–15; 1 Thessalonians 4:9–10.
61. Galatians 5:6, 22–23.
62. Galatians 5:24; compare Romans 8:9.

10

At Home in the Cosmos

Romans 8:14–39

The Root of All Evil

It is, *they* say, a dog-eat-dog world. In living by their creed, *they* lend it credibility.

Such a creed, and such a world, can see only weakness, not virtue, in practicing loyalty, kindness, or truthfulness.[1] Trust is mere naivety. *Dis*trust is essential to the goal of being numbered with the devourers rather than the devoured. Those who assert their own will at the expense of others are those most in tune with reality. Still, not even tyrants can feel at home in such a cosmos: sooner or later, they too will be its victims.

In the "Jewish-Christian" vision[2] of reality, there is goodness at the foundation of the cosmos, the source of its existence,

---

1. Indeed, such a vision of reality may well be thought to foster a hermeneutic of suspicion that dismisses all claims to virtue (which it cannot recognize) as screens for self-interest (which it descries everywhere).

2. For the sense in which I use the phrase, see chapter 1, note 7.

order, and life. Consequently, an obligation to goodness rests upon all moral beings: an obligation to trust, to affirm, and to pattern their lives according to the goodness at the source of their being. Moral codes may be of human construction. But the obligations of morality that such codes reflect (with limited and widely varied success) are built into the nature of the universe. The obligations may be embraced or defied. Their defiance may, among human beings, be universal.[3] They are not for that reason subject to change. Truthfulness is good. Loyalty is good. Kindness is good. Courage in pursuing any of these goods is itself good. And "good" cannot here be reduced to what we find pleasant or useful. There are times, after all, when the pursuit of such goods is neither pleasant nor obviously useful;[4] yet they remain good, and it is the duty of moral beings, in a universe built upon goodness, to embrace them.

Conversely, there can be evil in such a cosmos. Unless there is in the cosmos an inherent goodness that obligates human beings and is not of their own devising, "evil" can mean nothing more than "causing unpleasant sensations" or "hurtful to goals defined by human beings." Even the most heinous of atrocities can hardly be *evil* unless we can say why they *ought* not to take place. Such an ought, it seems, can only be found in a cosmos that is ultimately good—where there is rightness in all that affirms and evil in whatever disrupts and defies the good. The problem of evil can exist only in a world where goodness and evil are real, and where goodness is fundamental.

Evil is most emphatically a problem in the "Jewish-Christian" world. The abuse and murder of a child, the callous beating of the elderly in order to steal their pocket change, the atrocities of war—these things, the "Jewish-Christian" vision of the world

---

3. On this vision of reality (particularly in its Pauline form, marked by its perception of radical evil), many of the claims made by the various hermeneutics of suspicion can be allowed to be true: lamentably, self-interest does masquerade as virtue. The difference from the cynicism of dog-eat-dog hermeneutics lies partly in the adverb, partly in the absence of an ideological need to posit self-interest as the motivating force behind *all* the activities of *all* the Mother Teresas of the world.

4. One thinks, for example, of characters in Solzhenitsyn novels who refuse to comply with official deceit at incredible personal cost. The depictions were not the product of authorial fantasy.

insists, are more than distasteful. They are *evil*. They ought not
to happen. Nor, for that matter, are things as they ought when I
strike my child in anger, slander a rival, lust for what is not mine,
neglect the needy at my doorstep. Such vices may be common,
and commonly excused. In the "Jewish-Christian" world they
remain wrong, a distortion of what my life and the world were
meant to be.

On such a view, there would be no evil if the creatures whom
God has endowed with the capacity for moral goodness had

The problem of evil is a very real problem in the Bible.
The psalmists themselves frequently raise it:

Why, O Lord, do you stand far off?
   Why do you hide yourself in times of trouble?

In arrogance the wicked persecute the poor—
   let them be caught in the schemes they have devised.

For the wicked boast of the desires of their heart,
   those greedy for gain curse and renounce the Lord.

In the pride of their countenance the wicked say,
   "God will not seek it out";
   all their thoughts are, "There is no God."

Their ways prosper at all times;
   your judgments are on high, out of their sight;
   as for their foes, they scoff at them.

They think in their heart, "We shall not be moved;
   throughout all generations we shall not meet adversity."

Psalm 10:1–6 NRSV

---

maintained faith in him. One can be at home in the "Jewish-
Christian" cosmos, cared for by, and reliant upon, God's goodness. Were I to trust divine goodness as I ought, I would not be
tempted to lie, to cheat, to covet, to steal, to hurt, to become
jealous or bitter. The temptations result from my failure to trust,
my will to choose and fend for myself, my growing awareness
that much is beyond my control, my attempts to control things
nonetheless, the inevitable fears and frustrations bred by my

insistence on doing the immoral and the impossible. A vicious cycle of evil has been initiated by my failure to keep faith, by my will—in defiance of the obvious truth of my dependence upon God—to rule my own destiny and redefine *good* and *evil* to my own liking.

The Overcoming of Evil

In the "Jewish-Christian" vision, evil springs from bad faith toward an already-existing good. By the same vision, evil cannot survive forever. God, who is good, must oppose evil, overcome it, and—so *creative* is God's goodness—provide in the process redemption for his fallen creatures. Such is the biblical script where goodness is seen as foundational, but evil is nonetheless real.

In the Christian vision of the apostle Paul, God intervenes to put things right in the person of his Son, who lives the life of perfect trust and obedience that all were meant to live. All have not done so, however; and when God's Son takes upon himself the lot of Adamic humanity, he bears the brunt of its wickedness. He does so willingly, however, out of love for sinners.[5] In so doing, by the Father's will, he provides atonement for sin: through his death the bane of sin is exhausted.[6] His resurrection to new life opens, for those who trust in him, the possibility of sharing in that life,[7] and the hope that the One who raised Christ from the dead will one day do the same for Christ's adopted brothers and sisters.[8] Such is the divine salvation offered in Paul's gospel: divine in its confounding of human horizons,[9] in its unqualified abhorence of sin,[10] in the sheer selflessness of its love,[11] in its power to overcome sin and death.[12]

Paul declares that Christ has conquered sin and death. But before they can be eradicated forever, humanity's trust in God

5. Second Corinthians 5:14; Galatians 2:20.
6. Romans 3:25–26.
7. Romans 6:4, 8–11.
8. Romans 8:11, 29.
9. First Corinthians 1:18–25.
10. Romans 8:3.
11. Romans 5:8; Galatians 2:20.
12. Romans 8:3–4, 11; 1 Corinthians 15:54–57.

and his goodness must be restored through the proclamation of the gospel; otherwise the inevitable purging of creation from all that disrupts its goodness must wipe away humanity as well.[13] "Now is the time when God extends his favor; now is the day of salvation."[14] For a time, then, even those who belong to the new humanity "in Christ" must continue in conditions determined by sin: in bodies that are mortal, subject to deprivation, temptation, persecution.[15] Of their coming salvation, they enjoy for the present only a foretaste: the gift of the indwelling Spirit, making real the presence and love of God.[16] Otherwise their deliverance is a matter of hope that they do not yet see, a yearning—shared by all creation—for liberation from the corruption and havoc of sin. The life of the age to come may be incredibly blessed; but for the moment it is only in its birth pangs.[17]

And there is a fittingness in that. God's Son suffered the brunt of human evil because of his love for human beings; surely, Paul feels, Christians should count it a privilege if they in turn are allowed to suffer for his sake,[18] to be granted a share in his suffering.[19]

I consider that the sufferings of this present time are not worth comparing with the glory about to be revealed to us. For the creation waits with eager longing for the revealing of the children of God; for the creation was subjected to futility, not of its own will but by the will of the one who subjected it, in hope that the creation itself will be set free from its bondage to decay and will obtain the freedom of the glory of the children of God. We know that the whole creation has been groaning in labor pains until now; and not only the creation, but we ourselves, who have the first fruits of the Spirit, groan inwardly while we wait for adoption, the redemption of our bodies. For in hope we were saved. Now hope that is seen is not hope. For who hopes for what is seen? But if we hope for what we do not see, we wait for it with patience.

Romans 8:18–25 NRSV

13. See 1 Thessalonians 1:9–10.
14. Second Corinthians 6:2.
15. Romans 8:10, 23; 2 Corinthians 4:7–12.
16. Romans 8:23; compare Romans 5:5 and 8:15–16; 2 Corinthians 1:22; 5:5.
17. Romans 8:19–25.
18. Philippians 1:29; compare Romans 8:36; Galatians 6:17.
19. Romans 8:17; 2 Corinthians 4:7–12; Philippians 3:10.

Such suffering (Paul assures his readers), however severe (and Paul's own experience belongs in this category),[20] is nothing in comparison with the glory in store for those who love God.[21] They are, moreover, sustained in every circumstance by an overwhelming sense of God's love.

In *every* circumstance—Paul does his best to list them all.[22] In the process he mentions not only physical deprivation and hardship, danger, opposition, and death, but also whatever supernatural powers there may be ("angels," "rulers," "powers") that are malevolently disposed toward God's people. Although this is the only mention of such powers in the whole argument of Romans,[23] we can hardly conclude that Paul did not take them seriously. Undoubtedly he did, as others who share his vision have always done. There is no apparent reason why humans should be the only moral beings created by a God of goodness. Still, God, the Source and Sustainer of all life, is ultimately the only One with whom his creatures have to deal. No malevolent power is needed to explain human sin.[24] No force hostile to God can prevent his saving work.[25]

> Who will separate us from the love of Christ? Will hardship, or distress, or persecution, or famine, or nakedness, or peril, or sword? As it is written,
> "For your sake we are being killed all day long;
> we are accounted as sheep to be slaughtered."
> No, in all these things we are more than conquerors through him who loved us. For I am convinced that neither death, nor life, nor angels, nor rulers, nor things present, nor things to come, nor powers, nor height, nor depth, nor anything else in all creation, will be able to separate us from the love of God in Christ Jesus our Lord.
>
> Romans 8:35–39 NRSV

20. See 2 Corinthians 11:23–30.
21. Romans 8:18; 2 Corinthians 4:17.
22. Romans 8:35–39.
23. Unless we allow that Paul, in personifying sin in passages such as Romans 5:12, 21, and 6:12, has a more personal power (like Satan) in mind. The personification is not carried through with sufficient consistency, however, to make such a reading likely. Assurance is given in Romans 16:20 that Satan will eventually be overcome.
24. See Romans 1:18–3:20.
25. See Romans 8:33–34.

None can drive a wedge between God's people and God's love.[26] Powers of darkness are mentioned only to be dismissed as forces to be reckoned with.

In Paul's vision, encounters with distress, hunger, danger, and death cannot, in the end, determine human destiny. The decisive confrontation must be with divine love. It surrounds, sustains, embraces all. It offers all a home.[27] Those who respond in faith are adopted into God's family and know him as their *Father.*[28]

The early Christian emphasis on God as Father derives from the centrality of the theme in Jesus' own teaching.[29] The title "Father" conveys the idea that God is the source of all life. It presupposes as well his authority, and the duty of his children to submit to the Father's will.[30] Paul introduces yet a further motif to the theme of God's fatherhood when he declares that God's children will inherit—as his "heirs"—what God has set aside for their eternal enjoyment.[31]

> For all who are led by the Spirit of God are children of God. For you did not receive a spirit of slavery to fall back into fear, but you have received a spirit of adoption. When we cry, "Abba! Father!" it is that very Spirit bearing witness with our spirit that we are children of God, and if children, then heirs, heirs of God and joint heirs with Christ—if, in fact, we suffer with him so that we may also be glorified with him.
>
> Romans 8:14–17 NRSV

Nevertheless, the primary note is that of childlike trust in a benevolent father.[32] Ultimately, it is only with God that his

---

26. Romans 8:35–39.

27. Paul's language of "election" will concern us in the next chapter. The universal scope of God's love and redemptive plan is, for Paul, beyond question. See, for example, 2 Corinthians 5:14–15; Romans 11:32.

28. Romans 8:14–17.

29. Hence the preservation, in the midst of Paul's Greek text, of the Aramaic "Abba" (meaning "Father") used by his Lord (Romans 8:15; also Galatians 4:6). Compare Mark 14:36; and, on the theme, Matthew 5:43–48; 6:7–9, 32; 7:11.

30. First Corinthians 15:24–28; Mark 14:36; John 12:49–50; 14:28, 31; Hebrews 12:5–11.

31. Romans 8:17; Galatians 4:7.

32. It is tragic—on a host of levels—that the family experience of some does not lead them to link goodness and trust with the father-child relationship; in the early Christian language of God as Father, this association is instinctive and unquestioned (Romans 8:15; Matthew 7:11). *Maternal* solicitude was of

creatures have to deal, and his children need not approach him
with fear. The gift of God's Spirit assures them of his love and
enables them to address him with confidence: "Abba! Father!"

---

course proverbial for the biblical writers and offered a ready comparison to
divine care (see Isaiah 49:15; 66:13). It is nonetheless true that God is not
spoken of, or addressed, as "Mother" in the biblical texts, though frequently
as "Father." It does not follow that the writers of the Bible thought God to be
(sexually differentiated as) male. The language of sexual differentiation, of
"male and female," is applied to created species and linked (perspicaciously!) to
their propagation (Genesis 1:27–28). Such language is not used of God, nor are
divine creative acts thought of as sexual. (Not even the impregnation of Mary,
who bears God's Son, is portrayed as the result of a sexual encounter.) On the
other hand, God was no doubt thought of as "male" in a more limited sense:
the divine being was believed to demonstrate personal will and activity, and
humans naturally think of (and speak of) a personal being in male or female
terms—not both or neither. One may speculate why the (masculine) language
of fatherhood was deemed the more appropriate. The answer may lie in part
in that the ancients considered the male to be generative of new life, which the
female merely bore; and, in part, in that "fatherhood" was more suggestive of
the authority believed to be appropriately and benevolently exercised by the
Creator of all life.

   Again, the mention of "authority" requires the reminder that ancient horizons differed from our own. If (as many today are wont to claim) all human
good is self-defined, it may well seem to follow that all should be free to define
and pursue their own goals and paths to self-fulfillment. If, on the other hand,
as the "Jewish-Christian" vision maintains, human beings are *all* subject to the
same universal demands of goodness, truth, and love, then authority exercised
in keeping with these demands is far from problematic: mutual commitment
to common goals can allow the exercise of, and submission to, such authority
as the framework of a relationship of mutual love. (See, for example, John
5:19–23; 6:38; 8:28–29; 14:31; 15:9; Ephesians 5:21–31; Hebrews 13:17; 1 Peter
5:1–5). That authority can be abused for the selfish ends of those who wield it
was, of course, also recognized and the subject of frequent warnings (Ezekiel
34:1–10; Ephesians 6:4; 1 Peter 5:2–3; and elsewhere). Those who view the
world in the former way are liable to regard the structures of authority inherent in the latter as arbitrary and restrictive, if not oppressive. Those who view
things in the latter way are liable to see the competitive individualism and the
individualistic ideals of fulfillment characteristic of much contemporary thinking as introducing a tentativeness and instability into human relations that
prevent people from maturing in mutual trust and committed love. Whether
or not the two ideals can (or should) be combined lies beyond the purpose of
the present study to explore. It should at least be said that those who would
reproduce the message of the New Testament today devoid of its language of
authority run the risk of confusing Pauline ideals of freedom with what Paul
considers humanity's fundamental sin: the declaration of human autonomy
and the prioritizing of self-rule over the rightful claims of truth, goodness, and

Whatever may be their lot in a sin-scarred world, God's power and goodness guarantee that, in the end, "all things" will be seen to have "worked together" for their good.[33]

---

love. As we have repeatedly seen, freedom of choice is the highest ideal only in a very different vision of reality from that of "Jewish-Christian" faith.

33. Romans 8:28.

11

The Triumph of God in History

Romans 9:1–11:36

Meanwhile, what has become of Israel? Are God's chosen people still chosen? Or has God finally given up on the offspring of Abraham his "friend"?

If only as an academic question, the issue was bound to arise for Paul. Adamic humanity, as we have seen, is made up (for Paul) of God's creatures dependent upon him and determined not to admit it. From among them, God chose Israel to serve as a model and reminder of his universal rule. Himself a Jew, Paul needed no rehearsal to list the privileges God had granted to his people: they had been adopted as God's children; they had known the "glory"—the sensed and awesome presence of God; they had entered covenants with God that spelled out how they might continue to enjoy his blessing; they had been given God's law, a sanctuary where they could approach and worship him, and promises of future favors. Their forebears included those who had walked with God, and it was in their midst that the Messiah had been born. Truly God had been good to Israel.[1]

Still, for all of God's goodness to Israel, Adamic humanity—*including* Israel—remained estranged from him. None of these favors, Paul believed, had fundamentally altered Israel's own sinful bent, still less that of the pagan nations. God demonstrated his *tzedakah*—his faithfulness and goodness toward his creation—decisively and triumphantly in Jesus Christ, providing atonement for all of humanity's sins, deliverance from its bondage to sin and death, and reconciliation to himself. The proclamation of such a *gospel* (such "good news") *ought* to evoke a response of faith in God. The problem that Paul faces in Romans 9–11 is that most of Israel itself has not responded with the faith essential for salvation.[2] Does this mean that God's promises to Israel must go unfulfilled? That God's plan for humanity's redemption has met ironic frustration in the unbelief of his own people?

Paul raises the possibility only to summarily dismiss it.[3] Still, Israel's place in the divine scheme remains a quandary to be explored. And for Paul it is far from academic. His personal engagement with the fate of his people, his grief that they—though peculiarly favored—should prove so resistant to God's offered salvation, the conviction in his bones that God's goodness and redemptive purpose must nonetheless prevail in Israel as in all the earth: all these considerations require Paul to dedicate extended treatment to his people. In considering the main lines of his argument, we look first at how Paul views the condition of his Jewish contemporaries in relation to the divine agenda; second, at what Paul believes Israel's future to be; and third, at the place in his argument of human responsibility on the one hand, and the overarching divine will on the other.

God and Israel's Unbelief

In a nutshell, Paul believes that (1) Israel's lack of faith, though a source of personal anguish,[4] can hardly represent a breakdown

1. Romans 9:4–5.
2. Note Romans 10:1.
3. Romans 9:6; compare Romans 11:1, 11.
4. Note Romans 9:1–3; 10:1.

in God's plan, since that plan never entailed the inclusion of *every* descendant of Abraham in the community of blessing.[5] (2) Indeed, God himself is active and achieving his purposes in the *un*belief of Jews as well as in the coming to faith of Gentiles.[6] (3) Israel, of course, is active as well. In their case, Paul perceives a misguided adherence to the law and its "works" that keeps them from submitting, in faith, to the "righteousness" God offers in Christ. As a result, Israel turns a deaf ear to the proclamation of the gospel.[7] (4) Yet, while much of Israel remains as wayward as ever, a minority (or "remnant") has believed; and a faithful minority is all that is needed for God's relations with his covenant people to continue.[8]

1. The unbelief prevailing among Paul's Jewish contemporaries does not, for him, imply that God's commitment to his people has been frustrated. Nothing is new, Paul insists, in the current situation. The Israel that has enjoyed God's favor has, from its inception, been made up of a selection from among Abraham's descendants: Isaac, not Ishmael; Jacob, not Esau. What constitutes the community of blessing is not physical descent from Abraham but the divine promise. Hence, though God gave promises to Abraham's offspring, he is free to select the objects of the promise from among those descendants. Provided *some* Jews find seats in the pews of the church, the conspicuous absence of many of their compatriots does not call God's promise into question.

> It is not as though the word of God had failed. For not all Israelites truly belong to Israel, and not all of Abraham's children are his true descendants; but "It is through Isaac that descendants shall be named for you." This means that it is not the children of the flesh who are the children of God, but the children of the promise are counted as descendants.
>
> Romans 9:6–8 NRSV

2. Paul is prepared to go further. Far from frustrating God, Israel's unbelief represents a vital part of God's purpose: God

---

5. Such is the argument of Romans 9:6–13.
6. So Paul argues in Romans 9:14–29.
7. Romans 9:30–10:21.
8. So we may summarize Romans 11:1–10.

himself has "hardened" the hearts of his people.[9] Paul post-
pones until Romans 11 his discussion of what God means to
achieve in the process. For the moment, he is content to insist
that hardening people's hearts falls well within the prerogatives
of their Creator: has not the potter the right to turn one lump
of clay into a decorative vase, another into a pot that is merely
functional?[10]

Presupposed throughout the discussion is the estrangement of
Adamic humanity from God.[11] Paul proposes to disclose something of the mysterious way in which, in the course of history,
God operates to reconcile earth's estranged peoples to himself.
Paul never attributes the *origin* of humanity's bent toward sin to
an act of God. He does, however, claim (with ample precedent
in the Hebrew Scriptures) that God can steer humanity's existing bent toward sin in such a way that people choose *particular*
sins promoting his own purposes.[12] The upshot of this way of

9. The notion is, of course, a traditional one. See Isaiah 6:9–10; Mark 4:11–12;
John 12:37–40.

10. Romans 9:20–21, in which Paul alludes to Jeremiah 18:1–10.

11. This must be kept in mind when we read how, before they were even born,
Isaac and Jacob were chosen as objects of the divine promise, while Ishmael
and Esau were excluded (Romans 9:6–13). For Paul, Isaac *and* Ishmael, Jacob
and Esau must inevitably be part of that sinful humanity whose redemption
represents the ultimate goal of all God's promises. In Romans 9, Paul's concern
is to insist on God's prerogative to predetermine the role, whether honorable or
dishonorable, played by his creatures in his plan. In Romans 11, however, Paul
stresses that (1) God's former "calling" of Israel (including Isaac and Jacob) as
the community of his blessing, (2) his former excluding of non-Israelites (among
whom must be reckoned Ishmael and Esau) from that community, (3) his present "calling" of Gentiles into the community of his people, *and* (4) his present
hardening of Israel are *all* part of a strategic plan whose ultimate purpose is to
bring salvation to all the peoples of the earth (Romans 11:30–32).

12. In the Hebrew Scriptures, divine judgment of evil—itself regarded as
a good thing—is at times God's stated purpose in channeling existing human
hostility into particular sins: so, most notably, Isaiah 6:9–13. A comparable
case is found in 2 Thessalonians 2:10–12 (note, however, that some scholars
dispute the Pauline authorship of 2 Thessalonians). Romans 1:24–32 has been
interpreted along similar lines: God has channeled the energies of human beings who refuse to acknowledge him into deeds whose ugliness and vicious-
ness effect their own punishment. On the other hand, Paul's language (God
"gave them up" to such deeds) is perhaps more consistent with the view that
God simply left sinners to follow the path of their own sins, a path leading
inevitably to disaster.

thinking is that either the divine planner or the human actors can be seen as responsible for the activity in question: people, because they do the acts, and because their sinful actions are consistent with, and expressive of, their own rebellion against God's goodness; and God, because he has channeled human rebellion into specific acts that further his ends.

Thus, the pharaoh whose heart God hardened[13] was already the oppressor of God's people; but whereas ordinary common sense might have induced even Pharaoh to release Israel prior to their decisive redemption,[14] God "hardened his heart" so that Israel—and "all the earth"—might witness what a holy arm, laid bare, could accomplish.[15] The pattern is found elsewhere as well. When Joseph's brothers sold him into slavery, they were clearly giving vent to their own hatred;[16] but God channeled that hatred (which they could have expressed in other, less productive ways, including murder) into an action that served his own intention to preserve his people through an imminent famine.[17] When God made Samson's love of a Philistine woman a part of his divine plan, he was hardly forcing Samson to act out of character.[18] The same is true, presumably, of the rashness of Rehoboam that

13. Exodus 4:21; 7:3–5. But note that, in other texts, Pharaoh is said to harden his own heart (Exodus 8:15, 32). God's act of hardening is not thought to turn sheep into donkeys; it is seen merely as ensuring that donkeys do their kicking at a divine cue. As a result, Scripture can attribute a kick on cue with equal propriety to the willfulness of the beast or the wisdom of the Cue-Giver. And Pharaoh remains responsible for the sin of his hardened heart (Exodus 9:34).

14. See Exodus 10:7.

15. Exodus 7:3–5; 9:15–16; 10:1–2; Deuteronomy 7:17–19. Sinners such as Pharaoh are in any case "ready/fit for destruction" (Romans 9:22): God could appropriately destroy them at once. God is, then, entirely within his rights when he chooses instead to preserve the lives of people like Pharaoh so that they can serve as object lessons: on them, God can demonstrate his own hostility to sin on the one hand, and his readiness and power to save his people on the other. So Romans 9:22–23, essentially paraphrasing Exodus 9:15–16. The point of the passage is not to spell out the ultimate destiny of those "fit for destruction" whom God preserves as object lessons, nor how they came to be so fitted; Paul does not even address these issues. His concern is rather to explain how God can use sinful people ("fit for destruction") for his purposes—and to insist on God's right to do so.

16. Genesis 37:4, 18–28.

17. Genesis 45:5–8; 50:20.

18. Judges 14:1–4.

promoted God's intention to split the Israelite kingdom.[19] Paul explains Israel's present failure to respond to the gospel along similar lines.

3. Thus, though on one level Israel's current unbelief represents an outworking of God's purposes (to be explored in Romans 11), on another level it represents a fresh expression of Israel's perennial resistance against God, for which it remains responsible. At this point Paul interrupts his discussion of the divine program in history to outline his understanding of how Israel, in this instance, has gone astray.

Since Adamic humanity is characterized (for Paul) by its refusal to acknowledge God and submit to his will, Adamic human beings can experience God's favor only if *God* takes the initiative and shows them his mercy. God's blessing can hardly be a reward for people's God-pleasing activities if people are in fact incapable of pleasing God. The point is central to Paul's argument throughout these chapters. Isaac and Jacob, Paul has already insisted, were designated as the objects of divine favor before they were even born, before they had done *anything,* good or bad. The initiative, then, was manifestly God's: God was "calling" those whom he chose to be his people without regard for their "works."[20] Furthermore, when

> Even before [Isaac's twin sons] had been born or had done anything good or bad (so that God's purpose of election might continue, not by works but by his call) [Rebecca, Isaac's wife] was told, "The elder shall serve the younger." . . .
>
> [God] says to Moses,
> "I will have mercy on whom
> I have mercy,
> and I will have compassion
> on whom I have
> compassion."
> So it depends not on human will or exertion, but on God who shows mercy.
>
> Romans 9:11–12, 15–16 NRSV

19. First Kings 12:15. The author of the book of Acts explains the crucifixion of Jesus in similar terms: Jesus was betrayed by a people who had always opposed and persecuted God's servants (Acts 7:51–52), and he was executed by soldiers who were themselves "lawless" (2:23). They, in turn, were acting at the behest of two of those "kings of the earth" who have always opposed God and his Anointed (4:25–27; compare Psalm 2:1–2). Yet in all of these acts, each expressing the character of the actors, the predetermined plan of God was being accomplished (2:23; 4:26–28).

20. Romans 9:7–13.

God told Moses that he would show mercy to those to whom he himself decided to show mercy, he again made it clear that the bestowing of his favor owed nothing to the will or activity of those who received it.[21]

When Paul goes on to say that Gentiles who have *not* tried to win God's approval have nonetheless *found* such approval by faith,[22] the paradox is meant to draw attention to yet another instance of God's way of dealing with his sinful creatures. He has again granted his favor, not in response to human activity (the Gentiles were *not* active in seeking God's favor), but as a gift. Those who receive it as a gift are thereby moved to respond with faith—with trust, that is, in the God who has shown them his grace and goodness. But Israel, Paul claims, has not yet grasped this basic principle of faith. Instead, they are seeking to secure God's approval with "works" of their own, works done in obedience to the law. God offers to declare them "righteous" *apart* from any righteous deeds of their own, as an act of his own mercy, and because Christ died for their sins.[23] But rather than receive such "righteousness" by faith, Israel has continued to pursue the righteousness of an earlier divine revelation: the righteousness required by the Mosaic law.

> What then shall we say? That the Gentiles, who did not pursue righteousness, have obtained it, a righteousness that is by faith; but Israel, who pursued a law of righteousness, has not attained it. Why not? Because they pursued it not by faith, but as if it were by works.
>
> Romans 9:30–32 NIV

The law, to be sure, was itself a gift of God's goodness, a reminder of God's rule and of the demands it places upon his creatures. But Paul is convinced that the law did not—and could not—bring Adamic human beings to trust and obey God as they ought. The atonement of humanity's sins, and the transformation of humanity's rebellious bent into one of submission to God, has only been made possible by Christ Jesus. With Christ's

---

21. Romans 9:15–16.
22. Romans 9:30.
23. See the discussion of "Early Christian Perspectives" on atonement in chapter 5, and the discussion of faith in chapter 6, above.

coming, the law has fulfilled its divinely intended, though limited, function. Those who reject the gospel while continuing to pursue the law are credited with zeal; but the zeal, Paul claims, is misplaced.[24] In the end, the Jews of his day are proving—like their forebears—resistant to the purposes of God.[25]

> So too at the present time there is a remnant, chosen by grace. But if it is by grace, it is no longer on the basis of works, otherwise grace would no longer be grace.
>
> Romans 11:5–6 NRSV

4. Yet some Jews have believed: Paul himself is among them. In fact, the contemporary situation, in Paul's mind, has close parallels from the times of Elijah[26] and Isaiah.[27] In all three cases the existence of a faithful minority, "a remnant" chosen by God's grace, is sufficient evidence of God's continued commitment to Israel. The favored status of these few, Paul again insists, is the result of divine grace, not of their human "works."[28]

God and the Future of Israel

Denunciations of Israel's sins and warnings of pending doom dominate Israel's prophetic tradition. Still, the notion that judgment could represent the *final* stage of God's dealings with his people proved unthinkable: how could a divine initiative end in failure? Together with threats of judgment, then, Israel's ultimate restoration is a recurrent theme. So, too, is the insistence that the restoration owes nothing to the character or deeds of an intractable people and everything to the will of the God who restores them.[29]

Paul sees Israel's future in similar terms. At the moment, its people's hearts are hardened while non-Jews are given the

24. Romans 10:2.
25. The autobiographical element in Paul's depiction of Jews "zealous" for the law but hostile to the gospel—and hence to the purposes of God—should not be forgottten. See Galatians 1:11–16.
26. Romans 11:2–6.
27. Romans 9:27–29.
28. Romans 11:5–6.
29. See Ezekiel 20:5–44; 36:16–32; also 16:53–63; Isaiah 43:22–44:5; Micah 7:18–20. And note Psalm 79:8–9; Daniel 9:4–19.

opportunity to hear and to respond to the gospel.[30] But the hardening—and the attendant rejection of the gospel—is not permanent: when God's appointed time has come, Israel's Redeemer will banish its "impiety" and "unbelief."[31] Israel's "enmity" and "disobedience" toward the gospel[32] will give way to the obedience of faith, "and so all Israel will be saved."[33] In redeeming Adamic humanity, God proceeds by dividing and conquering the nations. For a time, the disobedience of Gentiles excluded them from God's favor while God treated the Jews with mercy. Now Israel's disobedience—or, from another perspective, the partial, temporary, strategic hardening of their hearts by God—gives Gentiles the opportunity to believe. "God has consigned all to disobedience, in order that he may show mercy to all."[34]

> Just as you [Gentiles] were once disobedient to God but have now received mercy because of [Israel's] disobedience, so they have now been disobedient in order that, by the mercy shown to you, they too may now receive mercy. For God has imprisoned all in disobedience so that he may be merciful to all.
>
> **Romans 11:30–32** NRSV

Does Paul mean that every Gentile and Jew will be saved? His words here certainly admit such an interpretation;[35] still, it probably goes beyond his intentions. Throughout the passage, faith is a prerequisite of salvation; and though divine mercy is universal in its scope, Paul knows well that unbelief

---

30. Paul does not say why Israel's unbelief is necessary if Gentiles are to be given the opportunity to believe. Perhaps he recalls that the Christian mission turned to Gentiles only after Jews proved resistant. Or his thinking may be steered by the conviction—common in his day—that God's kingdom would come when the Jews submit to God's will (note Acts 3:19–20): hence the need for Jews to *resist* God's will for a time so that Gentiles may be given an opportunity to believe *before* the kingdom comes and it is too late to repent. In any case Paul sees the scheme of history that he outlines in Romans 11 adumbrated in Deuteronomy 32:21 (see Romans 10:19; 11:11, 14).

31. Romans 11:20, 23, 26.

32. Romans 11:28, 31.

33. Romans 11:26.

34. Romans 11:32.

35. Note also Romans 5:15–19; 1 Corinthians 15:22; and compare Ephesians 1:9–10; Colossians 1:20.

can persist.[36] The grace of God can be "received to no purpose."[37] The claim that "all Israel" (or "Israel as a whole") will
be "saved" is intended as a contrast to a situation in which
a mere remnant has believed: it need not mean that every
individual Israelite will in the end submit, in saving faith, to
God.[38] And elsewhere, at least, Paul does speak of those who
"are perishing."[39]

What is clear for Paul is that God has not abandoned creation to be destroyed by sin. He has extended his mercy to all
of his creatures. In bringing salvation to all the peoples of the
earth, God has seen fit to deal in favor now with one nation,
now with another. For a time he excluded the pagan nations,
then hardened Israel's hearts in order that pagans might have
the opportunity to believe. Paul's vision ends with the triumph
of God's goodness among all nations, and gives way to praise of
the divine wisdom.[40]

The Role of God in Human History

In these chapters Paul deals with issues bound to arise for
those who adhere to the "Jewish-Christian" vision,[41] questions
to which that vision dictates no answer. Paul's own focus is on

36. Indeed, some may abandon the life of faith. Note the conditional force
of Romans 11:22–23. Similarly 1 Corinthians 15:1–2; and note 1 Corinthians
9:26–27; 10:1–5. In each case, since divine benevolence is presupposed, the
explicit condition on which salvation depends involves the human response to
God's goodness.

37. So 2 Corinthians 6:1. The whole passage (2 Corinthians 5:19–6:2) is in-
structive. God's purpose is to "reconcile the world to himself, not counting their
transgressions against them." To Paul (and others) God has entrusted the task
of communicating to the peoples of the world the divine offer of reconciliation:
"We beg you, on Christ's behalf: Be reconciled to God!" The entreaty receives its
urgency from the possibility of receiving, yet deriving no good from, the offer
of God's grace: "Do not receive [the offer of] God's grace in vain!" Hence the
repeated appeal: "Now is the time when God will accept you, now is the day of
salvation."

38. Note the allowance of exceptions at the time of Israel's restoration in
Ezekiel 11:17–21; 20:38.

39. First Corinthians 1:18; 2 Corinthians 4:3; compare Romans 2:5–10;
Philippians 1:28.

40. Romans 11:33–36.

41. On my usage of the term, see chapter 1, note 7.

Israel's resistance to the gospel. Yet human resistance to God's will takes many forms, and the relation between God's governance of his creation and the occurrence of deeds contrary to his will must appear problematic to any who would think through the implications of Jewish or Christian faith. In what follows I will briefly sketch several possible answers before suggesting, in only slightly greater detail, what appears to be the thinking of Paul.

1. If there is a before and after with God (as there undoubtedly is with his creatures), and if God plays no role in determining the decisions of human beings, then he may be thought to be ignorant of any particulars of the future dependent on humans exercising their will.[42] His plans, whenever they are dependent on the actions of moral beings, will at best be contingent.[43] God could not know that Adam would sin, though he could, presumably, prepare for the possibility that he would. Being God, he has the power to intervene in history at any point and impose his rule, rewarding some and punishing others; in that sense, history remains under his control. Still, his participation in history's course is minimal. The advantage of this way of thinking is that God is most evidently free of responsibility for the evil that humans bring upon themselves. He does not influence their actions—or even know of them in advance.

2. If there is *no* before and after with God, he may be thought to know all that (from a human perspective) is yet to transpire without being said to *cause* it. As a spectator on a hill sees but does not determine what lies ahead for a traveler below, so God, from the vantage of eternity, can know all that lies ahead for human beings without being the cause of its happening. Such knowledge obviously facilitates divine planning: God is in no doubt about what is going to take place. And God can still be thought to bear no responsibility for evil that he did not cause, though it is clear on this understanding that he has (fore)knowledge of its occurrence. His *control* of history is still limited to points of direct divine intervention.

42. On this view, if we are still to speak of divine omniscience, it will refer to God's knowledge of all that is logically knowable, which will *not* include future contingencies.

43. This is indeed suggested by the language of passages such as Jeremiah 18:1–10.

3. At the opposite extreme to the foregoing positions is the third view, by which God is thought to predetermine the activities of all his creatures, who are no more than puppets in his hands. He prescribes in advance the good and bad actions of all human beings, their faith or unbelief, their salvation or damnation. Humans may still choose their own actions, but God has so shaped their character and circumstances that their choices are really predetermined by him. Clearly, divine planning can here encounter no obstruction. Can we still speak of divine goodness? God (on this understanding) creates people whom he first causes to sin, then punishes for what they have done. A positive construal of the procedure might suggest that God intended to demonstrate that sin is a bad thing; the demonstration, in turn, might be considered one of the predetermined divine means for bringing about the predetermined faith of those predestined for salvation. Perhaps more difficult to account for on this view is the *sinfulness* of sin, for which God himself is the effective cause.

4. Somewhere between the second and third perspectives is a fourth position that sees humans as freely choosing their own activities at the same time as those activities are part of God's plans. By this view, God is in full control of history, shaping it to his own ends; but people remain free and responsible for what they do. If we cannot understand how the same action can be part of God's plan and yet freely chosen by the human being who does it, then that is *our* problem, not God's. How can we expect to comprehend the ways and resources of the Almighty?

And what of Paul's position? Any suggestions should be prefaced with the reminder that Paul nowhere explores these issues systematically. Even in Romans 9–11, Paul touches upon God's governance of history only as it relates to a particular, pressing problem: Israel's failure to respond to the gospel. Still (what I take to be) common *mis*constructions of Paul's understanding of divine governance require that we spell out what can be known on the subject.

1. Paul clearly attributes foreknowledge to God.[44] He is thus not among those who maintain the first position summarized above.

---

44. See, for example, Romans 1:1–2; 15:4; Galatians 1:15–16; 3:8.

2. Paul's language of divine election[45] and "hardening" rules out the second position (as well as the first): God's involvement in human activities, in these instances at least, goes beyond (fore)*knowledge* of decisions independently arrived at by human beings. Even the fourth position seems too weak a statement to account for God's acts in electing, or hardening, his creatures.

3. Does Paul think that God predetermines *all* human activities and choices (the third alternative above)? Some have so construed him. But the answer, as I read Paul, must be no.

In fact, Paul speaks of divine predetermination only in a few, limited contexts; in each case, he has special reasons for thinking such an explanation necessary. Adamic human beings, for Paul, *cannot* become God's people, or even respond to God's goodness with faith, unless God, acting on his own initiative, creates those possibilities; hence, the need for the "election" of believers. That God had predetermined Paul's apostleship seemed obvious to him: how else would such an opponent of the gospel ever have become its servant?[46] On the other hand, the divine hardening of Israel, in addition to being a scriptural motif that Paul would not have questioned, explained for Paul how Israel's unbelief could be a temporary condition that would not, in the end, exclude Israel from God's salvation. Paul exploited the divine hardening of Pharaoh (again, a traditional motif) to explain God's present hardening of Israel. In Pharaoh's case, a hostile ruler was made an object lesson of divine wrath and a key actor in the drama of Israel's redemption.

In all of these cases, human bondage and alienation from God are *presupposed* as conditions *requiring* God to predetermine certain human activities if he is to bring about salvation. It would be presumptuous to suggest, on the basis of these instances, that Paul thought God had predetermined *all* human activity. It would be still more presumptuous to use these cases, all illustrating God's redemptive purpose for human beings, as the basis for a claim that God predetermined as well the *sin* that brought about humanity's alienation from God in the first place.

And, in fact, Paul provides us with no justification for doing so. He speaks of the origin of humanity's bent toward sin fre-

45. For example, Romans 11:5, 7; compare also 8:29.
46. Galatians 1:11–16.

quently enough,[47] but never suggests a divine role in the calamity. Humanity's sinfulness is attributed solely to its own inexcusable behavior.[48] Paul can speak of God "giving [people] over" to their sins, and of the appropriateness of the abandonment in view of their choice to refuse him recognition.[49] Again, the language seems to rule out the possibility that Paul thought God himself was the ultimate *source* of human sinfulness.

4. On the other hand, it might well seem to follow that, if divine election is necessary for Adamic human beings to come to faith, then God must not have "elected" those who do not believe. God would still not be responsible for the sin that condemns them. And yet, by electing some to salvation (though they merit only condemnation) and not electing others (who also merit only condemnation), God would effectively be predetermining who is saved and who is not.

But though such implications may seem to follow, Paul does not appear to have drawn them. A number of Pauline texts speak of God's redemptive purposes as universal.[50] Statements of predestination to damnation are not to be found. Furthermore, a number of texts indicate that divine grace can be resisted, and even that members of the Christian community may prove faithless and be lost.[51] None of this suggests that Paul thought the ranks of the saved and the perishing have been fixed from all eternity.

In short, Paul clearly reckons with divine foreknowledge. He thinks that humanity bears full responsibility for its alienation from God and potential condemnation. He believes that God does, on occasion, channel human hostility to goodness into particular acts of sinfulness that further his purposes. Paul declares that God has chosen and called those who believe. He affirms

47. For example, Romans 1:20–21; 5:12–19; 1 Corinthians 15:21; 2 Corinthians 11:3.

48. Romans 1:20; compare 3:19.

49. Romans 1:21–28.

50. Romans 5:15–19; 11:30–32; 1 Corinthians 15:22; 2 Corinthians 5:14–15, 19; and note (though the Pauline authorship of these epistles is disputed) Ephesians 1:9–10; Colossians 1:20.

51. Romans 8:12–13; 11:22–23; 1 Corinthians 3:16–17; 9:26–27; 10:1–12; 15:1–2; 2 Corinthians 6:1; Galatians 5:2–4; 6:7–8; 1 Thessalonians 3:5.

that God's redemptive purposes are universal. He also indicates that God's grace and call can be resisted, to damning effect.

Nowhere does Paul try to reduce his convictions in these matters to a logical system. He believes that God has demonstrated his *tzedakah* in Christ Jesus, the climax of a divine plan that included both Abraham and Moses. Yet even that demonstration and that perceived design provide, not unambiguous answers to all questions, but only grounds sufficient for trusting the goodness and the wisdom—surpassing mortal understanding—of the Creator, Redeemer, and Judge of all humankind.

12

On Living the Good Life

Romans 12:1–16:27

Not infrequently, I find myself confronted with a ballot containing a list of names I do not recognize, none of which I can even vaguely link with a face, an interest, or a policy. If I proceed to mark my ballot anyway, I play a part in the election of my representative. But I can hardly be said to have exercised my right to *choose* my representative, since no meaningful choice has been made. *Choice* implies preference. Faced with alternative courses of action, I *choose* the one that appears to me most satisfying, most likely to bring me closer to some goal I have set, most beneficial or pleasing to someone I love, most in keeping with principles I cherish. In each instance, I express something I *value* in my choice. Where this is not the case, where no judgment based on values that I hold is involved, I have not made a meaningful human choice. The outcome could just as well have been determined by the flip of a coin.[1]

---

1. A special case merits mention here. Often I must decide between alternatives that express competing values I do in fact hold: whether, for example, I

If we only make real choices when we see some value in what we choose, then we do not *choose* our values themselves—unless we have already recognized something valu*able* about them.[2] In this respect, our values resemble our beliefs, or the trust we put in other people. I can choose to act (for any number of reasons) as *if* I believed a certain proposition, even though in reality I am not convinced of its truth; but I can truly *believe* only what I find believ*able*. (Put differently: I cannot truly be said to believe a statement that I find less than believable.) I can choose to act (for any number of reasons) as *if* I trusted the elderly man next door, even though I am not persuaded that he is reliable. I may, for example, lend him my lawn mower even though he lost my weed cutter, because I value good relations with my neighbor. But I can truly *trust* only those I deem to be trust*worthy*. (Put differently: I cannot truly be said to trust a person I think less than trustworthy—though I may act as though I did and hope for the best.) Similarly, I can choose to act (for any number of reasons, some quite cynical) as *if* I placed value on compassion, even though in reality I care for no one but myself. But I can only make compassion one of the values I will live by if I already sense that compassion is valu*able*, or good. (Put differently, I cannot truly claim to *value* compassion if I sense nothing *good* about it.)

In short, I cannot simply choose my values any more than I can simply choose my beliefs, or those in whom I trust. What I believe I must *find* believable; it is not believable because I choose to believe it. What I trust I must find trustworthy; it is not trustworthy because I choose to trust it. What I value I

---

will tell the truth or save my skin. I make a meaningful choice if I decide that one value is more important to me than the other and act upon that *preference*. If, on the other hand, I can see no basis for favoring one value above the other, and my decision is based on nothing more than the equivalent of a coin toss, my choice is less than meaningful. In such a case, however, it does at least affirm a value that I hold.

2. It follows that a life for which freedom of choice is the *only* value that is recognized would be a life devoid of meaning. Freedom to choose is only of value if the choices that we are free to make are meaningful. Yet to make a *meaningful* choice, we have to value, in addition to the freedom to choose, *something* about the alternatives we choose. Children in whom no value but self-determination is inculcated will be utterly unable to decide for themselves on a meaningful course of action.

must *find* valuable, or good; it is not valuable because I value it. *What* I find valuable, believable, or trustworthy will depend, in part, on my experience, in part on my understanding of life as a whole.

One need not be able to spell out and defend one's values in order to live by them; many do so instinctively. Some, indeed, live by values that they could not defend, since the values that they exhibit in practice have no place within their own stated vision of reality. People have always embraced in practice things that, in their thinking, they regard as wrong. Conversely, people may in practice display a keen sense that certain things are right while others are wrong even though, in theory, they dismiss such distinctions as mere conventions of society.[3] But such split personalities—people who live by principles that have no place in their stated view of life—can hardly serve as our ideal. More integrated personalities act on values that directly reflect their worldview, whether or not they themselves could show the linkage. If, in addition, they are able to communicate to others their vision of reality in a compelling way and convince them, as a result, to adopt principles of behavior consistent with their vision, they qualify as moral thinkers and teachers.

For two thousand years the legacy of Paul has been that of a moral thinker of extraordinary impact. He himself was utterly enthralled by a vision of reality, and his captivation proved contagious. But he also succeeded in spelling out principles of behavior appropriate to that vision. To this point the vision itself has been the focus of this book. We conclude, as Paul concludes Romans, by noting briefly the principles of behavior that Paul derives from it.

Discussions of Pauline ethics tend to focus on the related issues of freedom and the law.[4] We may begin by observing that the notion of the good is more fundamental to his moral thought. A brief look at what he means by "the good" will follow, then a summary statement of how Paul envisages life in its service.

3. See the discussion of "Doubts about Sin," in chapter 3, above.
4. The Mosaic law is intended (as usually in Paul) by unqualified references to "the law."

The Obligation of Goodness

The obligation to goodness is, in Paul's mind, universal; not so, however, the obligation to law.

1. In Romans 2, Paul repeatedly distinguishes between Jews, to whom the law was given and who are responsible for its observance, and Gentiles, who neither have nor will be judged by the law. Yet the criterion of judgment, he insists, is the same for both:

> God will give to all according to their deeds. To those who persist in doing good and so pursue the path that leads to glory, honor, and lasting blessedness, he will give eternal life. But for those who are self-seeking, who disobey the truth and obey what is wicked, wrath and anger are in store. Distress and anguish will come upon all who practice what is evil: Jews in the first place, but also Greeks. Glory, honor, and true prosperity will be the reward of all who practice what is good, Jews in the first place, but also Greeks. There is no prejudice with God.[5]

Jews and non-Jews alike must practice what is good. To be sure, God has favored Jews with a concrete statement of what the good requires. Yet that knowledge, Paul adds, is useless unless matched by good behavior.[6] Gentiles, though without the law, are subject to the same moral demands. Note the direction of Paul's thought: the good is not good *because* God commands it in his law; rather, the law spells out, for the benefit of Jews, what is the good that is required of all human beings.[7] Paul later claims that those who do no evil to their neighbors have thereby fulfilled the law.[8] Again, the presupposition is not that the commands of the law *make* things good or evil, but that they *embody* the good. Hence, those who do what is good and avoid evil, whether or not they are familiar with the law, in fact fulfill the law's demands.[9]

---

5. Romans 2:6–11.

6. Romans 2:17–24.

7. Note also what Paul says about the law in Romans 7:12. In the immediate sequel, Paul writes as one who wants to do "the good" but cannot (Romans 7:18–19, 21). Again, the law is said to be good *because it corresponds* to the good that Paul acknowledges people ought to do (Romans 7:15–16).

8. Romans 13:10.

9. See also Romans 2:25–29. Excluded from consideration in both Romans 2 and Romans 7 are the laws that Paul, together with Jewish tradition, saw as

In short, human obligation to do the good is universal. The law of Moses is merely the form in which Jews encounter that obligation.

2. Indeed, Paul declares that sin was rampant before the law was even given.[10] The law brought definition to existing sin, increased its visibility, gave its condemnation legal grounds. But even without law, in the period between Adam and Moses, human beings were bound by an obligation to the good—which they defied.

> I do not understand my own actions. For I do not do what I want, but I do the very thing I hate. Now if I do what I do not want, I agree that the law is good. . . . I delight in the law of God in my inmost self.
>
> Romans 7:15–16, 22 NRSV

3. Paul believes, moreover, that Christians have "died to the law."[11] Its hegemony he confines to humanity "in the flesh": to rebellious human beings the law serves as a reminder of their creaturely limitations and obligations. Inevitably, it exacerbates their rebellion. From that way of life, and from the law that provoked and condemned it, Christians have been set free.

But the obligation to goodness remains. Paul portrays the good life in Romans 12–16 with scarcely a mention of the law.[12] When he goes on to say that Christians may eat all foods and that they do not need to consider any day as more sacred than any other,[13] he speaks in obvious disregard of much that the Mosaic law prescribes.[14] But Christians are still bound to do the *good*.

---

binding only on Israel. See the discussion of "The Place of Law in Deuteronomy" in chapter 4, above.

10. Romans 5:12–14.

11. Romans 7:5–6; compare Galatians 2:19.

12. He notes only (Romans 13:8–10) that those who live in love thereby fulfill what the law demands.

13. Romans 14:1–9, 14.

14. Though Paul believes, as we have seen, that the Mosaic law contains commands that embody the universal requirements of goodness, he also thinks that it includes other demands serving a more limited function among Jews (see note 9, above). Christians, in his view, are *not* subject to the law since (1) the latter demands do not apply to them, (2) the former demands are not dependent on the law of Moses for their validity, and (3) the law was given to confront and condemn the rebellion of humanity "in the flesh."

Detest what is evil, cling to what is good.[15]

Do not be overcome by evil, but overcome evil with good.[16]

Do what is good, and you will receive praise from your rulers. For they are servants of God for your own well-being, promoting what is good. But if you do what is evil, you have cause to fear.[17]

I want you to be wise when it comes to the good, innocent when it comes to evil.[18]

Ultimately, then, Paul's understanding of the good life is not determined by compliance with law, nor is it distinguished by limitless freedom. The mark of the good life is its orientation toward *the* good.

The Definition of the Good

In none of these passages does Paul spell out his understanding of "the good." Still, its Pauline definition should (by this time!) be straightforward. Two ways in which Paul summarizes the Christian's moral responsibility provide the necessary clues.

1. In 1 Thessalonians 2:12, Paul urges his converts to behave in a manner *"worthy* of the God who calls [them] to his own kingdom and glory." Paul also challenges the Philippian Christians to conduct themselves in a way *"worthy* of the gospel of Christ."[19] The good life, then, involves a "worthy," or "appropriate," response to God's demonstrated goodness.[20]

2. At several points in his letters, Paul sums up human ethical responsibilities by referring to the duty to love others.[21] Closely related are the charges to his readers to live for the good of oth-

15. Romans 12:9.
16. Romans 12:21.
17. Romans 13:3–4.
18. Romans 16:19.
19. Philippians 1:27.
20. The same principle is at work when Paul bases his moral appeals to believers on what God has already done for them: "Because God has done *x,* you should (by way of response) do *y.*" A good example is Romans 12:1.
21. Romans 13:8–10; Galatians 5:14. Nor should we forget 1 Corinthians 13, his famous hymn on love.

ers rather than please themselves.[22] When Paul depicts moral obligation in these terms, he is merely spelling out our appropriate response to God's goodness: those who experience and are transformed by God's goodness respond appropriately with love for those whom God loves, and with a desire to see God's good purposes realized in their lives.[23] Furthermore, living with the best interests of others in mind should be possible, even natural, among those who trust God to care for their own.

For Paul, then, the guiding principle of the good life is the duty to love others. Needless to say, love, for Paul, is to be expressed in ways that are informed by, as they represent an appropriate response to, the goodness of God in creation and redemption.

> Owe no one anything, except to love one another; for the one who loves another has fulfilled the law. The commandments, "You shall not commit adultery; You shall not murder; You shall not steal; You shall not covet"; and any other commandment, are summed up in this word, "Love your neighbor as yourself." Love does no wrong to a neighbor; therefore, love is the fulfilling of the law.
>
> Romans 13:8–10 NRSV

The Good Life

In Romans 12–16, Paul speaks of three contexts in which Christians must live the good life: in (a non-Christian) society; within the community of believers; and before God.[24] Here we must be content to note briefly the behavior that Paul thinks appropriate in each of these contexts.

1. According to Romans 13:1–7, God has ordained that society be governed by authorities with the power to reward well-doing and to punish evil. Humans prosper when society is stable and

22. Romans 15:1–3; 1 Corinthians 10:24, 33; Galatians 6:2; Philippians 2:4.

23. Note Romans 15:1–3, 7; Philippians 2:4–5. The point is clearest in Ephesians 5:2, though the Pauline authorship of the letter is disputed. Compare also 1 John 4:7–21.

24. In Romans Paul does not discuss a fourth context—that of the family—though he does mention sexual immorality and disobedience to parents in Romans 1, where he sees them as expressing humanity's resistance to the goodness of God's created order. See the discussion in chapters 3–4, above.

the distinction between goodness and evil is recognized and maintained. Concern for human well-being is therefore appropriately shown in respect for such authority and the due payment of taxes and tributes.[25]

Christians are to show their goodwill toward their neighbors by sharing their good times and bad: "Rejoice with those who rejoice, weep with those who weep."[26] They are to be careful to maintain both a reputation for personal integrity and—to the extent it depends on them—good relations with others.[27] If others mistreat them, the tone of their response is to be determined not by the ill will of their persecutors but by the goodwill and love that they have themselves experienced in Christ.[28] Justice should be left in the hands of God, who will ultimately purge his creation of irredeemable evil.[29] The task of God's people is to seek to redeem the evil they encounter by responding in love, to "overcome evil with good."[30] All these instructions follow naturally and appropriately from Paul's vision of reality.

> The night is far gone, the day is near. Let us then lay aside the works of darkness and put on the armor of light; let us live honorably as in the day, not in reveling and drunkenness, not in debauchery and licentiousness, not in quarreling and jealousy. Instead, put on the Lord Jesus Christ, and make no provision for the flesh, to gratify its desires.
>
> Romans 13:12–14 NRSV

25. Paul does not discuss what should be done when rulers fail to promote good or to curb evil. Romans is not, after all, a systematic treatise on life in society, but a letter to a particular community at a particular time. Paul must have felt that existing circumstances required no more than the broadest statement of principle.

26. Romans 12:15.

27. Romans 12:17–18.

28. Romans 12:14, 17.

29. Romans 12:19.

30. Romans 12:21. Romans 12:14, 17–21 provide a close parallel to the words of Jesus in Matthew 5:38–48. "Overcome evil with good" is, in effect, a more prosaic way of saying "Turn the other cheek" (Matthew 5:39). It seems also to represent Paul's interpretation of the obscure words that close the quotation from Proverbs (25:21–22) given in Romans 12:20. In light of Romans 12:21, the "coals of fire" experienced by an enemy who is treated with kindness seem to be pangs of remorse that lead to repentance.

Christians, however, are not to procure good relations with others by sharing a lifestyle of loose living, contentiousness, or jealousy. License, self-assertion, and a preoccupation with self-interest are the marks of humanity's rebellion against the divine order of love. They cannot survive the ultimate triumph of the good. Christians are to align their behavior unequivocally with the good.[31]

2. The good life is not lived in isolation, not even in a solitary pursuit of the good. A worthy response to God's goodness includes participation in the community of the redeemed.

> For as in one body we have many members, and not all the members have the same function, so we, who are many, are one body in Christ, and individually we are members one of another. We have gifts that differ according to the grace given to us . . .
>
> Romans 12:4–6 NRSV

Within the community, there is to be mutual respect, aid for the needy, hospitality: these are obvious expressions of the Christian duty to love.[32] But most of what Paul says in this context addresses concerns raised by the inevitable diversity within the community of believers. People are not to consider themselves better than others or to keep from associating with them because of an inflated self-image.[33] The community is like a body with different parts, each performing a role important to the functioning of the whole. The ability to carry out a function is itself a gift of God's grace. It demands to be used, as intended, for the good of the whole. Some believers are to convey messages from God, others to exercise administrative leadership; some to encourage, others to attend in tangible ways to the physical needs of the community. Whatever one's area of service, it must be performed wholeheartedly.[34]

In these chapters Paul gives only one ethical issue extended treatment: it pertains directly to diversity within the community of believers and was, presumably, of local concern in Rome.[35] He

31. Romans 13:11–14.
32. Romans 12:9–13.
33. Romans 12:16; note also 12:3.
34. Romans 12:3–8.
35. For what follows, see Romans 14:1–15:6.

discusses the principles at stake in a general way that leaves us in some doubt about the particulars; but the most likely background, in my judgment, is as follows.

The Christian community in Rome included many non-Jews who had never observed the Mosaic food and festival laws, and perhaps some Jews who had ceased their observance. Both shared Paul's conviction that all foods may be eaten by the one who receives them with thanks, as gifts from the hand of God. But also within the community were Jewish Christians who kept a more restrictive diet, either because they considered themselves still bound by the laws of torah, or (and Paul's language perhaps favors this second alternative) because a lifetime of observance had left them with scruples that did not disappear when they adopted Christian faith. All were Christians. All intended to express in their eating their devotion to God. But the differences in eating habits threatened to divide the community.

Paul *pre*scribes mutual acceptance, on the principle that those whom God has accepted, his people must be prepared to accept. He *pro*scribes condemning each other on the principle that God is the only competent judge of his servants. He tells those whose conscience forbids them to eat certain foods to follow their convictions. Not that the foods are inherently "unclean." But everything Christians do is to express their confidence in God's goodness and favor, and no such confidence can be felt by people who eat what they sense they ought not to be eating.

Paul's vision of the good determines his response to those with a more robust conscience as well. In principle, he writes, they are free to do what their conscience permits: even eating, when accompanied by an acknowledgment of our dependence on God, becomes an act of appropriate service. On the other hand, that same act of eating becomes mere self-indulgence if done without consideration for others. If, by eating, those with a robust conscience cause grief to those more scrupulous than they, or if, by eating, they tempt the more scrupulous to violate their scruples, then the robust have failed in their paramount duty to love. In these cases, pleasing God requires self-sacrifice. The sacrifice is minimal, however, for those whose focus in life is not on food and drink but on right living, peace, and the joy of knowing God's presence.

Some practices and teachings are directly counter to God's purposes in creation and redemption, expressive rather of self-interest than of service to Christ. Goodwill toward all is not to be confused with naivety. The believers' mature understanding of the good and of its implications should keep them from being led astray.[36]

3. Those captivated by a sense of God's goodness will want to give themselves to his service. In temples throughout the world, animals were dedicated to various deities and sacrificed on altars. Paul adopts language from this practice: "Present your bodies as a sacrifice that is living, holy, and pleasing to God; this is your spiritual[37] service."[38] All that Christians do, in society as well as within the community of believers, is to reflect their desire to carry out God's will.[39]

At no point is the difference between Pauline horizons and those of contemporary Western society more apparent. Within the latter, individual freedom and self-fulfillment are for many the highest ideals. For Paul, living to please oneself is a bad thing, and insistence on self-determination is calamitous. Conversely, obedience, service, self-sacrifice, and even slavery—when God, or the Lord Jesus, is the master—are *positive* terms, the marks of a life worth living.

> I know and am persuaded in the Lord Jesus that nothing is unclean in itself; but it is unclean for anyone who thinks it unclean. If your brother or sister is being injured by what you eat, you are no longer walking in love. Do not let what you eat cause the ruin of one for whom Christ died. So do not let your good be spoken of as evil. For the kingdom of God is not food and drink but righteousness and peace and joy in the Holy Spirit.
>
> Romans 14:14–17 NRSV

36. Romans 16:17–20.

37. The term here almost means "figurative": the metaphorical "sacrifice" of the believer's body that is given to God's service is compared to the literal sacrificing of animals carried out in temples. At the same time, the Greek word suggests that dedicating oneself to God's service is a "reasonable" thing for humans to do.

38. Romans 12:1.

39. Romans 12:2, understood as a statement of principle that encompasses the specific instructions to follow.

The differences can be exaggerated, of course, or the point of divergence misconstrued. Moderns, too, know that the furtherance of a common cause may require some to exercise leadership, others to follow. Our world, too, witnesses much self-sacrifice that is motivated by love. But obedience and service in these cases are required by particular circumstances. What many of us lack today is a vision of reality that would prescribe *service* as a way of life: a sense that, undergirding all our lives, there is a goodness that is both rewarding and worthy of human devotion.

If human existence is an accident, if the functioning of the cosmos is merely mechanical, if the language of right and wrong is rooted in nothing deeper than human convention, if the world is but the indifferent stage on which we give shape to our lives, then we may well resent any attempt to curtail our freedom and self-determination. If, on the other hand, human existence is a gift of love, if the functioning of the cosmos is providential, if language of right and wrong reflects our appropriate and inappropriate responses to reality, and human existence—indeed, all creation—has been cursed by human self-assertion; and if, moreover, Jesus Christ represents God's refusal to abandon his willful creatures to their sin; if Christ demonstrates the goodness of a life lived in obedience to God, his self-sacrificial death atones for human wrongdoing, and his resurrection makes possible eternal life in communion with God as a member of his redeemed people: if all these basic convictions of Paul are true, then (perhaps even people today would agree) there can be no prouder title than that claimed by the apostle—a "servant of Jesus Christ."[40]

40. Romans 1:1.

Index